Coaching
by
Values

Coaching
by
Values

*A guide to success in the life of
business and the business of life*

SIMON L. DOLAN

iUniverse, Inc.
Bloomington

Coaching by Values
A guide to success in the life of business and the business of life

iUniverse books may be ordered through booksellers or by contacting:

iUniverse
1663 Liberty Drive
Bloomington, IN 47403
www.iuniverse.com
1-800-Authors (1-800-288-4677)

Because of the dynamic nature of the Internet, any web addresses or links contained in this book may have changed since publication and may no longer be valid. The views expressed in this work are solely those of the author and do not necessarily reflect the views of the publisher, and the publisher hereby disclaims any responsibility for them.

ISBN: 978-1-4620-3880-0 (sc)
ISBN: 978-1-4620-3881-7 (ebk)

Library of Congress Control Number: 2011912552

Printed in the United States of America

iUniverse rev. date: 07/30//2011

Other books by Simon L. Dolan

Managing by Values (with Salvador Garcia and Bonnie Richley)
Stress, Self-Esteem, Health and Work
Beyond: Business and Society in Transformation (with Mario Raich)

I dedicate this book to the greater **Dolan** *&* **Landau** *family for the values they have shared with me and the great inspiration they provided for completing this book. First, to my brother* **Avishai** *Landau, who exemplifies values in forging honest, transparent, dedicated, and quality relations in all aspects of his life; he is the best partner one could have asked for. To his son* **Ran** *Landau, who developed the idea of the Value Juggler (which is used on the cover of this book and on our card games). To my son* **Tommy** *Dolan, who proposed the creative subtitle for this book. To my daughter* **Keren** *Dolan, who showed that diversity is not an empty word by marrying* **Kamal** *and bringing me my first Indian grandchild.*

I also dedicate this book to my late parents, **Lola** *&* **David** *Landau, who instilled in me the values that made me whoever I am.*

 **Preface**

This is a rather long preface. If you are not interested in my life story and how I got involved in values and coaching, or if you are pressed for time, go straight to the essence of the book.

This preface is about how I came to write this book. It is about my evolution as a scholar and a human being. I've written more than 47 books (including new editions of older books)—and scores of academic articles—in numerous languages on several management and psychological subjects. About a year ago, I decided to set aside the academic style of writing for which I was trained (and perhaps brainwashed) to write a different kind of book. This is the most personal of all my books; I wrote it for you.

You do not have to be an academic or an expert in any of the disciplines I discuss here. You don't even have to be a professional coach. I try to use straightforward language and not assume too much knowledge in any one area. I have attempted to maintain rigor, and most of what I say in this book is backed up by scientific evidence, but I do not claim that the content is highly scientific nor do I pretend that it is all-inclusive. Whether you are a scientist, a coach, a manager, a concerned mother or father, or anyone else who wants a richer, more meaningful life, I hope you will find my messages and the logic behind them compelling, convincing, and sound.

The book is not intended to be a recipe, or a panacea, for resolving all of life's problems. It is also not intended to be an instant guide to becoming a coach although the methods and tools I provide can be used for self-coaching. It is a particular life philosophy—and the methodology I've developed from that—that has been evolving in my head following years of observations, readings, and reflection. You may disagree with some of my messages; I expect that and understand it. My hope is simply that you will find many of the ideas useful and applicable to your own life and the lives of those you impact. I also hope the book will serve as an eye opener—an appetizer for your own reflection—and perhaps a catalyst for altering your course of action and your lifestyle.

I will try to convince you that you can better understand what makes you tic, what motivates you, and what makes you happy by identifying your values and aligning them with your goals. Values, for many people, are only words. And for the vast majority of people, these words are insignificant in their daily lives. What a pity. I have discovered that when you understand your values (regardless of how and why they have emerged), analyze their consequences on your daily behavior, and see more clearly how they affect (or might affect) your daily life, you can make more informed choices that can enhance your mental and physical well-being, leading to a happier, more fulfilling life.

Writing this book was a result of a long journey. Back in the early 1980s during and immediately following my doctoral studies, I was concerned with individual well-being and dedicated all my energy to studying it from an emotional and physical perspective. My research in the 1980s in Minnesota and Montreal dealt with the phenomena of stress—specifically, chronic stress. I was trying to understand its origins, its nature, and its consequences in work situations. I am still pursuing scientific research in this complex, multidisciplinary, and fascinating field as part of my role as the Future of Work Chair at ESADE.[1]

During the 1990s and early 2000s, I became concerned about the sustainability of organizations. I was intrigued by what makes some organization far better places to work than others and how this translates into economic success. This led me to write several books on how to manage people in organizations in the twentieth and twenty-first

---

[1] See, for example: Dolan, S. L. & Arsenault, A. (1980). *Stress, Santé et Travail* (Preface by Hans Selye). Université de Montréal; Dolan, S. L. (2006). *Stress, Self-Esteem, Health and Work*. London: Palgrave Macmillan; Dolan, S. L., & Arsenault, A. (2009). *Stress, Estime de soi, Santé Travail*. Montréal: Presses de L´université du Québec.

centuries and how to develop a unique culture that will distinguish the excellent organizations from the not-so-excellent.[2] Luckily, the books were published in many languages and were read by politicians and business leaders around the world.

I've spent more than 15 years touring the globe explaining my ideas and sharing the models and methodologies that I have constructed to implement them at conferences, speeches, and seminars. I have savored the success of these books primarily because they've given me the opportunity to meet talented world business leaders and often to be instrumental in effecting changes in them and their organizations.

I don't know if you believe in serendipity, but I believe it was truly a moment of serendipity when I met a colleague at ESADE, Dr. Mario Raich as the twenty-first century was approaching. We engaged in multiple conversations and debates. We discussed macro business and world issues ranging from world economy to world ecosystems and world values. Mario convinced me that we all need to be concerned about the sustainability of the world and that we should look at problems from a global and holistic perspective. In his gentle and spiritual manner, he insisted on the difference between a "change" and a "transformation" (losing the capacity to go back). I began thinking about the threats that this presented globally, and felt a real discomfort. This led to a joint venture; Mario and I coauthored the book *BEYOND: Business and Society in Transformation*,[3] which has already been translated into several languages including Spanish, Portuguese, German, and Polish. The message in the book is very clear: "We are entering a new era of transformation of business and society, and we are not ready for it."

I decided it was time for me to come out of my comfort zone and *do* something before it is too late. My training is in management and psychology, and as you can probably tell already, I have spent most of

---

2   See, for example: Dolan, S. L., & Schuler, R. S. (1994). *Human Resource Management*. Ontario, Canada: Nelson Thomson Learning; Garcia, S., & Dolan S. L. *Dirección por Valores*. Madrid: McGraw-Hill; Dolan, S. L., Garcia, S., & Richley, B. (2006). *Managing by Values: Corporate Guide to Living, Being Alive, and Making a Living in the 21st Century*. London: Palgrave Macmillan.

3   Raich, M., & Dolan, S. L. (2008). *Beyond: Business and Society in Transformation*. London: Palgrave Macmillan.

my life in academia and in management circles. My scientific papers and scholarly books were read only by a handful (perhaps hundreds or thousands) of academics. Being convinced of the urgency of our global situation, I felt I needed to reach broader audiences. Because I am versed in multiple cultures and speak numerous languages, I arranged to have my nonacademic books published in other languages, and the results were encouraging. Some of the books were translated into Chinese, French, German, Hebrew, Polish, Portuguese, Spanish, and more. But this alone was not enough, so I started developing educational games that would bring awareness of values to children and parents.[4] The card game I developed with my brother Avishai is now available in five languages and four versions. Despite very poor marketing efforts, it is growing in popularity. The enthusiastic reactions and comments I've received from users give me great joy.

While doing the research for *Beyond*, Mario and I came across the writings of Riane Eisler, who has written numerous best-selling books that are making a real impact on world view. In her most recent book,[5] published in 2008, Riane advocates abandoning the frequently used paradigm of dominance and replacing it with a paradigm of partnership and care. We forged a fruitful synergy with Riane that led to our co-writing several papers and a new, future-oriented book that is currently in preparation.[6] My global journey, meetings with world business and political leaders, collaboration with leading academic scholars, experience with the coauthors of my book *Managing by Values* (Salvador Garcia and Bonnie Richley), my consulting and coaching experience, and the reinforcement I've received from many colleagues, students, and administrators at ESADE have all helped shape my ideas and at the same time have deepened my belief that it is time to share "Coaching by Values" with the larger world. It offers people something they can do **here and now** to enhance their general well-being, by applying the concept to themselves (self-coaching) or by helping others in need (professional coaching).

---

[4]   See: www.learning-about-values.com

[5]   Eisler, R. (2008). *The Real Wealth of Nations, Creating a Caring Economics.* Berrett-Koehler.

[6]   Raich, M., Eisler, R., & Dolan, S. L. (2011, forthcoming). *Beyond History: Roadmap Toward a Sustainable Future* (tentative title, book in preparation).

I want to single out three people who have been most helpful in bringing this book to completion. Scott Moodie, my doctoral student at ESADE, was a source of inspiration. We share a deep curiosity about values, well-being, and the potential for technology to help us harness these concepts. He read earlier versions of the book and provided instrumental feedback and ideas, which I've incorporated into the final manuscript. Avishai Landau, my brother and partner in the design, production, and distribution of the values card games, was my first fan and admirer and has been a constant driver, pushing me to complete the writing. And finally, I will be always in debt to George-Thérèse Dickenson. We began our relationship professionally as I needed a good copy editor and she came highly recommended, but as time evolved she became enmeshed in the message and gradually has become a real partner. Her comments, suggestions, modifications, and quality control made this book whatever it is now.

I hope that you will enjoy reading and learning from this book as much as I enjoyed writing it.

> Values are words embedded with significant meaning;
> When they are sorted and
> Translated into concrete behavior aligned with our goals and objectives
> And shared with people about whom we care,
> They become a tool for a very powerful guide to

Success in the life of business and the business of life

Simon L. Dolan
Barcelona & Montreal, July 2011
E-mail: *Simon.Dolan@ESADE.edu* or *Simon.Dolan@learning-about-values.com*

Contents

Original contributions by some of
the foremost management-paradigm-
breakers and coaching gurus:

- *Michael Arloski*
- *Richard Barrett*
- *David Caruso*
- *Riane Eisler*
- *Michele Hunt*
- *Dave Ulrich*

Introduction:

The Story of CBV

"Coaching by values" and "managing by values" were born many years ago. In fact, humans have been using them ever since we first attempted to organize work. Only recently, however, has the significance of values been part of the global discussion about coaching and management. As a part of my contribution to this conversation, I crafted the formal methodologies Managing by Values (MBV) and Coaching by Values (CBV). I created them after a series of internal debates based on my academic work, my experiences as a professional consultant, and the evolution of my own personal life.

In the 1970s, I experienced a "management reality shock" that forced me to rethink the basic paradigms underlying most methods of dealing with and managing people, in organizational and nonorganizational contexts. While completing my doctoral work in Minnesota, I was involved in a small-scale qualitative study of patients at the Mayo Clinic who had survived their first heart attack. I discovered that more than 90% of these patients attributed their condition to stress at work. At about the same time, I began to notice the constant push of senior managers in organizations to increase productivity without taking larger issues into consideration. They completely ignored such critical questions as, Why do we work? What is the purpose of our enterprise? Are profits and power the supreme objective whereby any means justify ends?

This led me to see the essential paradox of modern societies: We have better hygienic conditions and medical care, better working conditions, and more means to provide care and enjoy leisure, but many of us kill ourselves trying to achieve or conform to unrealistic goals. Today people are not only killed by physical guns but also (and likely more often) by psychological ones: the threat of losing one's job (or partner), the pressure to perform at superhuman levels at work for prolonged periods, and so on. I realized that we were witnessing the emergence of a new type of toxicity. It has no color and no odor but causes tremendous suffering and illness, and at times it even leads to death.

I started to question deeper issues of life and death and the meaning of life (work life and personal life) in general. I also started to search for a new definition of success. I was convinced that in any organizational or social context (e.g., partner, family, community, and the like), success had to include the well-being and prosperity of both the organization and the individuals who make it up. To begin to examine this two-dimensional (organization and individual) approach to success, I developed a four-quadrant model (see exhibit I.1).

Exhibit I.1: A two-dimensional definition of success

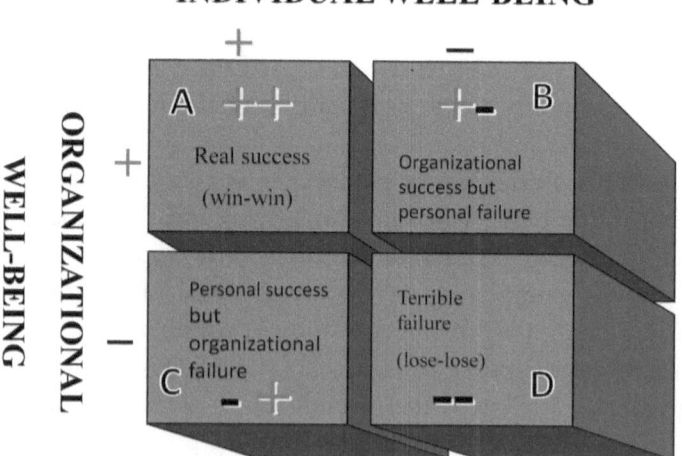

Quadrant A represents a win-win situation. The most clearly problematic situation is quadrant D, where not only does a person perform poorly, but his or her health becomes affected as well. Quadrants B and C are also problematic zones in which either individual health or organizational health is affected. The question that this simple two-dimensional model of success suggested to me was, Can we create a culture in which people's well-being is not endangered (or is just minimally affected) or is even enhanced and in which their performance contributes to the culture's well-being?

I believed the answer was yes, it must be possible for people to perform well while keeping their personal mental and physical health intact; in fact, I hypothesized, this could lead to even better performance and make for a healthier and more robust organization. I thought long and hard about this, and realized that a journey toward enhanced well-being would begin with values. And thus this simple model became the foundation for Managing by Values and Coaching by Values, methods, tools, and techniques that can be used by professional coaches and for self-coaching, in organizations and in life.

Values are predispositions to our behavior; they are associated with beliefs and norms. I recognized that if we can understand our values, organize them in a coherent logic (a logic that makes sense to us), and align them with our goals (life, work, family, and so on), we can get closer to the state of utopia known as optimal well-being. To begin to create a model for this, I had to better understand the multidimensional core element that is values.

A value is a belief, standard, mission, or principle that has worth and is useful.[7] Values are deeply held beliefs regarding what is good, correct, and appropriate. They help us determine how we should be and act if we are to be of worth to ourselves and useful to society. Values can range from the commonplace, such as the belief in hard work and punctuality, to the more psychological, such as self-reliance, concern for others, and harmony of purpose. Once we identify the values that are meaningful to us, we can develop strategies for implementing them. But toward what ultimate goal?

---

[7]   As we will see later in the book, values, beliefs, and norms are not exactly the same in terms of their etiology—i.e., there is a sequential development within each person and within societies from beliefs to values, which are then expressed on a social level as norms.

What exactly is "optimal well-being"? Of course it varies from person to person, organization to organization, and culture to culture. But to create models flexible enough and specific enough to help people attain the state as they see it, I had to get more clarity about its universal elements. To arrive at a new definition, I needed to know more. I had to go beyond a general understanding of "well-being" and happiness by starting at the beginning.

Philosophers and social researchers have defined happiness and well-being in a variety of ways. The largest divide is between the hedonic view, which emphasizes pleasant feelings and avoidance of pain, and the eudaimonic view, which emphasizes doing what is virtuous, morally right, true to one's self, meaningful, and growth-producing. The hedonic approach focuses on one's subjective well-being, which is usually seen as having two correlated components: a) one's judgment of life satisfaction—overall or in specific domains such as relationships, health, work, and leisure—and b) one's having a preponderance of positive feelings and relatively few negative feelings. In contrast, the eudaimonic approach focuses on self-validation and self-actualization and suggests that a happy or good life is doing what is right and virtuous, growing, pursing important or self-concordant goals, and using and developing one's skills and talents, regardless of how one may actually *feel* at any point in time.[8] I decided to take an eclectic approach in developing Coaching by Values, an approach that would combine both.

And finally, Coaching by Values had to be a dynamic concept and a methodology susceptible to growth, able to change as the world changed while staying true to its core. It has grown and evolved dramatically in the past several years based on the feedback of thousands of practitioners and academics. I am sure that in the future it will evolve further (in chapter 5 I look at some possibilities for this, particularly, adding a spiritual dimension). But underlying this concept and this book is my belief that values are the most fundamental element of our road to success in the life of business and the business of life.

---

[8] For an excellent review on happiness at work, see: Fisher, C. D. (2010). Happiness at work. *International Journal of Management Reviews, 12,* 384–412. And for life happiness, I really recommend: Ben-Shahar, T. (2007). *Happier: Learn the Secrets to Daily Joy and Lasting Fulfillment.* McGraw-Hill.

Through self-coaching, or in dialogue with a professional trained coach, you can improve the alignment of your values with your goals and achieve a more meaningful life and enhanced happiness. When your vision of reality finally matches reality itself, your actions will consistently produce the best possible results. This isn't just an individual journey; it involves all humankind. Social creations like democracy, human rights, global sustainability, and right to food, education, partnership, and caring are developments in the ongoing process of values clarification.

Coaching by Values is not just another fancy gadget or chimerical technique. In both its application to the individual and to larger cultures or contexts, it requires serious thought and mindful action. It gets to the heart of what it means to have a good life and a creative, robust, and versatile organization. It is integral to the entrepreneurial spirit and leadership necessary to imaginatively tackle the challenges confronting the world today. In the twenty-first century—at least at this point—no one can claim there is an oversupply of true entrepreneurs and true leaders either in our organizations or among the organizations themselves.

Today, almost 40 years since I experienced my "management reality shock," things have not changed. We hear reports of an epidemic number of suicides among the professional employees of the giant French company France Telecom and a wave of suicides of ordinary workers in China after being stuck in repetitive, routine, and boring jobs. We are living in a twilight period in which people are experiencing a growing sense of futility and numbness in every sphere of life, not just at work, but in the family, in politics, and in economics. We see our environment decaying—or being destroyed—around us. We are facing constant chaos. Things are changing sporadically and unexpectedly at an ever-increasing pace.

I cannot provide any guarantees, and it may not be the last word, because there is no last word, but CBV addresses real human needs, it has real meaning, and it makes sense on both the individual and organizational level. If you use the methods I've developed to audit, sort, and prioritize your values, align them with your goals, and follow them with concrete actions, embodying them in the smallest details of your life and work, the result will most likely be a more fulfilling and harmonious life, which in turn generates an inner satisfaction that increases your physical and mental well-being and energizes your state of mind. This is my definition of success.

Chapter 1

A Coaching Kaleidoscope

1.1 Everyone can be a coach

Everyone can develop a personal life and find or create a work situation imbued with creativity, innovation and playfulness. Everyone can find relative happiness, despite the dour predictions of politicians and pundits. And anyone can be a coach. You may be a professional coach, or perhaps you are a manager who is eager to engage employees. Maybe you just want to improve your own life or that of you and your spouse. Maybe you want to help your colleagues—or your group or team—define goals and move toward their fulfillment effectively and efficiently.

In this chapter, I will present an overview of the types of coaching available and the primary schools of thought in the field. I will explore what it means to be a coach—and how coaching is different from mentoring, training and counseling.

But primarily, this book is about values; it is about life values, work values, community values, world values and all the values that power our lives and our organizations. It is also about value alignment. And in chapters 2, 3, and 4, I'll introduce you to a way of thinking about values and present a framework, methodology and tools for value reengineering—Coaching by Values.

1.2 What is coaching?

Coaching is the art of bringing out the greatness in people in a way that honors the integrity of the human spirit. It is both an innate human capacity and a teachable skill.

Coaching is not a new discipline that has suddenly been invented. It is probably as old as the first Stone Age spear-throwing competition, and has always been a natural part of life for people everywhere. It is used by millions of great parents who love their children unconditionally, believe in them, and put their own needs aside to nurture their potential and encourage them to be great. It is used by thousands of great business leaders who make an effort to develop their people, not by abusing their power, but by believing in them, challenging them, supporting them, giving them more positive than negative feedback and making sure they take care of themselves.

The term *coach* originated in the sports field in the late 1880s and became a well-known sports profession that's taken many different forms over the years. Even today, the term *coaching* often produces a mental image of a football or basketball coach. Depending on what the coach actually does, this analogy may or may not be adequate. The head coach is in fact usually a general manager or chief executive officer responsible for running an entire program. The image of a quarterback coach or offensive line coach who enables others to play through teaching is somewhat more accurate.

The first use of the term *coaching* to mean an instructor or trainer arose around 1830 at Oxford University as slang for a tutor who "carries" a student through an exam, but only in the past 15 years or so has an individual been able to purchase coaching services outside the sports or performance arena. The evolution of coaching has been influenced and enhanced by many other fields of study including personal development, adult education, psychology (sports, clinical, developmental, organizational, social, and industrial), and other organizational or leadership theories and practices.

In its modern application—as a new way of working with people within different contexts—coaching is a relatively new discipline. Although its emergence as a popular profession is unclear, according to some sources, it began in the United States in the late 1980s. Only a decade or two after its quick rise to popularity, however, the practice (at least in terms of application to management) appeared to fall into disuse for a time. These were the days of the full-blooded management-training programs and marathon groups.

The current field of coaching is the result of the convergence of several developmental strands dating back as far as the 1940s. Only in recent times has it has been recognized as field with a largely cohesive set of principles, knowledge, and skills. Since the mid-1990s, it has coalesced into a more independent discipline. The proliferation of coach training schools—close to 100 in the United States alone—and the establishment of the International Coach Federation[9] (ICF) have led to a dramatic increase in the number of professional coaches worldwide. The ICF, one of the largest nonprofit professional coach associations, has more than 5,000 members spanning 179 chapters in 30 countries. It has drafted a set of core competencies for coaching that are now recognized as the fundamental competencies for this profession globally.

According to British sources, the most important developments in the profession of coaching, especially in the business world, include the following:

---

[9] Davison, M., & Gasiorowski, F. (2006). The trend of coaching: Adler, the literature, and marketplace would agree. *Journal of Individual Psychology, 62,* 188–201.

- Tim Gallwey's 1974 book *The Inner Game of Tennis* proposed a novel, psychological approach; he claimed that as well as being prepared physically and technically, a player must be prepared psychologically to attain peak performance. Gallwey, a tennis coach, observed that the opponent in one's head is greater than the one on the other side of the net.[10] From this observation, he pioneered the facilitative approach to sports coaching, a discipline that had previously been solely a skills-based learning experience with a master in the sport.

- In 1992, Sir John Whitmore, a motor racing champion, published *Coaching for Performance* in which he developed one of the most influential models of coaching, the GROW model (Goal, Reality, Options, Will). He has since become a guru in the business world and has continued to refine his model. The latest version of the GROW model appeared in the fourth edition of *Coaching for Performance*, published in 2009.[11]

- In the 1990s, the Western world went into recession and corporate downsizing became the rage. It may have seemed good in theory, but did not take into account human needs. This left managers and leaders in highly stressed environments without support, increasing the need for individuals and organizations to continuously develop. This need for performance maximization contributed to the upsurge in coaching.

- When businesses first began to rely on coaches, they were brought in as often for poor performers as for high performers (often to deal with performance issues when the manager did not want the hassle or conflict). Now, however, the vast majority of coaching is aimed at high-level performers rather than remedial cases. Coaching today is for the high performer, top talent, and those leading an organization.

---

[10] Gallwey, W. T. (1974). *The Inner Game of Tennis* (1st ed.). Random House.

[11] Whitmore, J. (2009). *Coaching for Performance: GROWing Human Potential and Purpose*. London: Nicolas Brealey.

What is the process of coaching all about?

Coaching is for people looking to work actively toward making tangible changes. The process of coaching refers to the activity of the coach in developing the coachee's abilities, especially those required for making the sought-after change(s).

Coaching tends to focus on an existing problem that an individual wishes to resolve (move away from) or a specific outcome that the individual wishes to achieve (move toward). In both cases, the coach aims to stimulate the coachee to uncover innate knowledge and/or skills so he or she can achieve a sustainable result. Coaches will normally make sure the specific learning can be successfully reapplied by the coachee to other problems in the future. The structure and methodologies of coaching are numerous as we will see later, but all coaching approaches have one unifying feature: *They are predominantly facilitating in style,* that is, the coach mostly asks questions and challenges the coachee to learn from her own inner skills. The coaching process is underpinned by the coach's established trust in the coachee.

It is important to note here that—despite their focus on questioning and dependence on trust—coaching is not therapy, and coaches are not therapists; psychological intervention is outside the scope of the coach's tasking. The problems and outcomes that coaches address are rooted in current contexts with aims for the future; they do not have emotional etiology or baggage from the past—in other words, the coachee has the resources she needs to make reasonable progress at the time she seeks coaching. As Vicki Brock said in her 2008 doctoral dissertation on the history of coaching,[12] "Most definitions [of coaching] assume an absence of serious mental health problems in the client and that coaching's purpose is to effect some kind of change using similar knowledge, skills, and techniques."

During the process of coaching, a coach may find that a coachee is so unfamiliar, inexperienced, or ignorant of an area that requires sharp focus if the coachee is to achieve his or her stated aim(s) that the coach will need to impart knowledge and examples to the coachee. So there may be an education component in which new skills or information are shared, but a coach always returns to the facilitation style.

---

[12] Brock, V. (2008). *Grounded theory of the roots and emergence of coaching* (Unpublished doctoral dissertation, p. 13). International University of Professional Studies, Maui, Hawaii.

Even though the practices and professional disciplines of coaching are diverse, the effects of coaching's questioning on the coachee are fairly consistent and almost universally observed along a continuum of levels of challenge—regardless of the specific coaching approach: At the lowest level, questions excite intellectual processes in the coachee, and the coachee is observed to be alert and responding quickly. When questions are more demanding (for example, "Imagine what it might be like to be the person you are experiencing relationship difficulties with"), the coachee will be observed to be actively alert, thinking and leaving pauses between some responses. The highest levels of challenge cause the coachee to access deeper structures in his or her experience than those accessible by rapid, intellectual recall. This deeper information may include feelings (emotions), pictures, auditory experiences, and metaphors.

Coaching is most often performed on a one-to-one, face-to-face basis, but it may involve telephone or web-based sessions. Sometimes it is conducted totally via phone or web-based interaction. The coach may assign homework to be done between sessions as a way of beginning to help a client integrate changes into daily realities.

Some coaches are wholly coachee-centered and responsive to the coachee's objectives and needs. Other coaches set up a program or "learning journey" that the coachee must follow over a specified period of time. Some coaches or coach-training schools prescribe a certain number of models or a "toolkit" to guide the coach. There are also many generic coaching pathways to help coaches know where they are in a coaching process; these are used by both independent coaches and training schools (including academic and commercial schools and those affiliated with associations). Multiple coach-training schools and programs are available, allowing for many options (and sometimes causing confusion) when an individual decides to gain "certification" or a "credential" to apply to the coaching industry.

Core competencies for coaches

Regardless of his or her approach, a professional coach must have the following core competencies:[13]

---

[13]   I modified these from ICF (International Coach Federation) list as presented in: Davison, M., & Gasiorowski, F. (2006). The trend of coaching: Adler,

- **Knowledge:** Knows the background of coaching and can distinguish coaching from counseling, therapy, training, and consulting; has familiarity with the specialist vocabulary of coaching, and knows the criteria for testing both process and outcome goals.

- **Relationship skills:** Builds a relationship of respect and trust with the coachee; works so the coachee is accountable for the coaching process and the tasks he or she agrees to in that process; creates an equal, synergistic partnership with the coachee.

- **Listening skills:** Fully attentive during the coaching process; able to listen and provide support to the coachee's self-expression; focuses on the coachee's agenda and not his or her own; and finally, is in touch with and pays attention to his intuition.

- **Self-management skills:** Keeps his or her own perspective and does not become enmeshed in the coachee's emotions; evaluates and distinguishes the different messages the coachee gives; is sensitive to and calibrates the coachee's nonverbal signals. "Calibration" is more critical in some coaching schools of thought (such as NLP) than in others, as we will see later.

- **Inquiry and questions:** Helps the coachee define the present situation in detail; asks powerful questions that provoke insight, discovery, and action; uses different perspectives to reframe and clarify the coachee's experience; supports the coachee's growing self-awareness; and finally, makes the coachee aware of incongruence between his or her thoughts, emotions, and actions.

- **Feedback skills:** Shows the coachee areas of strength and elicits and supports his or her inner resources; shows the coachee where habits are holding her back and supports any change she wants to make; celebrates the coachee's successes.

---

the literature, and marketplace would agree. *Journal of Individual Psychology, 622,* 188–201.

- **Goals, values, and beliefs:** Works with the coachee to overcome limiting beliefs; explores the coachee's values and helps coachee become aware of them; does not impose his or her own values; works with the coachee to clarify his goals and check that they are congruent with the his values; clearly requests actions that will lead the coachee toward his or her goals.[14]

- **Designing actions and tasks skills:** Creates opportunities for ongoing learning for the coachee; gives appropriate tasks for the coachee to challenge him or her and move her forward toward her goals; helps the coachee to develop an appropriate, measurable action plan with target dates; provides challenges to take the coachee beyond her perceived limitations; and finally, holds the coachee accountable for the mutually agreed tasks and actions.

Differences between coaching and mentoring, managing, and training

Advocates of coaching claim that the role of coaches and the processes they employ are very different from those used in consulting and other helping professions. Although there is some overlap between coaching and mentoring, coaches are supposed to help clients build skills, while mentors shape mental attitudes. Moreover, while instructors and teachers train for immediate tasks, coaches are supposed to accompany achievements. Here is an encapsulation of the responsibilities of managers, trainers, and mentors:

- Managers need to ensure that people actually do what they know how to do

- Trainers need to teach people to do what they don't know how to do

---

[14] All competencies are important. However, I believe that in relative terms, the most important competencies are those of identifying values, analyzing incongruences between values and goals, and steering or aligning respective behaviors. In later chapters, I will explain "Coaching by Values," which focuses and enlarges on these.

- Mentors need to show people how the people who are really good at doing something do it

Coaches seem to be none of the above. They are supposed to help people identify the skills and capabilities that are within them (inner skills) and enable them to use these to the best of their abilities, increasing the individual's independence and reducing reliance.

However, as we will see later, increasingly companies are expecting their managers to have some coaching skills that they can use to guide their employees and help them realize their potential.

A survey conducted in 1998 noted the principal differences between mentoring and coaching. These differences were found primarily in the areas of focus, role, relationship, source of influence, and arena, as shown in exhibit 1.1.

Exhibit 1.1: Differences between mentoring
and coaching in work context

	Mentor	**Coach**
Focus	Individual	Performance
Role	Facilitator with no agenda	Specific agenda
Relationship	Self-reflecting	Perks (come with the job)
Source of Influence	Perceived value	Position
Arena	Life	Task related

SOURCE: Adapted from http://www.coachingandmentoring.com/Articles/mentoring.html.

The Chartered Institute of Personnel and Development (CIPD) also distinguishes between coaching and mentoring, as we can see in exhibit 1.2. It is helpful to understand these differences because although many of the processes are similar, they are generally delivered by individuals with different qualifications and different relationships with their clients.

Exhibit 1.2: Differences between mentoring and coaching

Mentoring	Coaching
Ongoing relationship that can last for a long period of time	Relationship generally has a set duration
Can be more informal and meetings can take place as and when the mentee needs some advice, guidance, or support	Generally more structured in nature and meetings are scheduled on a regular basis
More long term and takes a broader view of the person	Short term (sometimes time-bounded) and focused on specific development areas/issues
Mentor is usually more experienced and qualified than the mentee and is often a senior person in the organization who can pass on knowledge and experience and open doors to otherwise out-of-reach opportunities	Coach is generally not required to have direct experience of the client's formal occupational role unless the coaching is specific and skills-focused
Focus is on career and personal development	Focus is generally on development and issues at work
Agenda is set by the mentee, with the mentor providing support and guidance to prepare the mentee for future roles	The agenda is focused on achieving specific, immediate goals
Mentoring revolves more around developing the mentee professionally	Coaching revolves more around specific development areas/issues

SOURCE: Adapted from the Chartered Institute of Personnel and Development (CIPD).

1.3 Types of coaching

I titled this chapter "A Coaching Kaleidoscope" because of the variety of focuses, approaches, and paradigms involved in the coaching process. Having outlined the basic coaching process and the competencies an effective coach must have, I'll present—at the risk of leaving out some importance facets of the discipline—a few of the major types of coaching, each of which has its own paradigms, gurus. and leaders. In the next section (1.4), we will turn to principal schools of thought in the coaching field.

By "types of coaching," I'm referring to the environments in which coaching takes place and the types of client involved. "Business coaching" takes place within an organizational context and may involve an individual, a team (e.g., a department or a group working together on a project), or the organization as a whole (e.g., a small business or nonprofit). "Executive coaching" focuses on an individual executive in a business setting. "Life coaching" is a one-to-one relationship with a client regarding personal goals. "Family coaching" is coaching within the family; it may involve a couple, parents, teens, or other family members.

Business coaching

Business coaching is always conducted within the constraints placed on the individual or group by the organizational context. Interestingly, a good business coach need not have specific business expertise and experience in the same field as the person receiving the coaching to provide a quality business coaching service. Business coaches often help businesses grow by creating and following a structured, strategic plan to achieve agreed-upon goals. However coaches are not consultants; business analysis is outside the realm of their activities, although some coaches may have a background in this field.

Multiple organizations train professionals to offer business coaching to business owners who may not be able to afford the prices of large coaching firms. Business coaching, reported the National Post, is one of the fastest-growing industries in the world, following the IT industry. According to MarketData Report in 2007, about 40,000 people in the United States work as business or life coaches, and the $2.4 billion business coaching market is growing at about 18% per year. The Australian Institute of Management said that as of 2006, 70% of its member companies were hiring coaches for business coaching.

Coaching is not a practice restricted to external experts or providers. Many organizations expect their senior leaders and middle managers to coach their team members toward higher levels of performance, increased job satisfaction, personal growth, and career development. These organizations back up their expectations with training in coaching skills, access to feedback tools, and/or descriptions of specific coaching behaviors in their leadership competency models. In many organizations, human resource managers are gaining expertise either in coaching or in selecting and subcontracting business coaches for their top talents.

Executive coaching

This is a special case within the business coaching model. Executive coaching is the one-to-one relationship between a coach and a client based on the intrapersonal goals of the client within the organizational context.

Whereas coaching was once viewed by many as a tool to help correct underperformance, today, as I mentioned earlier, it is becoming much more widely used to support top producers. In fact, in a 2004 survey by Right Management Consultants (Philadelphia), 86% of companies said they used coaching to sharpen the skills of individuals who have been identified as future organizational leaders.

Although both the organization and the executive must be committed to coaching for it to be successful, the idea of engaging a coach can originate either from human resources and leadership-development professionals or from the executives themselves. In the past, it more often came from the organizational side. But given the growing track record of coaching as a tool for fast movers, more executives are choosing coaching as a proactive component of their professional life.[15]

Many approaches and models are used for executive coaching. According to The Linkages Best Practices in Coaching Survey, which included participants from 19 countries, the majority of organizations that use coaching use it for developing leaders with one or a combination of the following models or concepts: 360-degree feedback (62%), action learning (48%), supervisor interview (48%), peer interview (40%),

---

[15] For more information, see Michelman, P. (2005). What an executive coach can do for you? Harvard Working Knowledge Archive (http://hbswk.hbs.edu/archive/4853.html).

behavior modeling (35%), Appreciative Inquiry (32%), and shadowing (29%).[16] We will look at some of these later.

Life coaching

Life coaching, or personal coaching, is a future-focused practice designed to help clients determine and achieve personal goals. It has its roots in executive coaching, which itself drew on techniques developed in management consulting and leadership training. Life coaching also draws inspiration from disciplines including sociology, psychology, positive adult development, mentoring, career counseling, and other types of counseling. An individual coach may employ such techniques as values assessment, behavior modification, behavior modeling, goal-setting, and others.

The process of life coaching is accomplished by first gaining a thorough understanding of an individual's personal traits, needs, and wants, then developing an understanding of the goal(s) or aim(s) to be achieved, and finally formulating action plans, review processes, and measurable outcomes. Goals may be in almost any realm of life, including personal, business, educational, relationship, and health.

Some people trace the origin of life coaching to Thomas Leonard, a former financial planner who came on the coaching scene in about 1988 from the business world. While working for Werner Erhard, he began doing life planning work on the side, creating a course titled "Life Creates Your Life." With others, he assembled some basic ideas about life planning, applied to them knowledge derived from the business and financial arenas and launched the industry we now call life, or personal, coaching. He organized his concepts into a curriculum for training coaches that could be implemented around the world via telephone. He also set up his own company and founded a coaching university (www.coachu.com).

Between 1998 and his sudden death at 47 in 2003, Leonard authored six coaching-related books: *Working Wisdom, The Portable Coach, Becoming a Coach, Simply Brilliant, The Coaching Forms Book,* and *The Distinctionary.* He is widely credited with having codified, popularized, and globalized the coaching discipline. Interestingly, while he was collaborating with thousands of people, he held within the broader vision

---

[16] Morgan, H., Harkins, P., & Goldsmith, M. (Eds.) (2005). The Art and Practice of Leadership Coaching. Wiley.

of these efforts a vision of himself as highly impactful, a leader, and one who was competitive against others doing similar things; he was intensely competitive and intensely collaborative at the same time.

Psychology and life coaching may seem—at first look—to be pretty much the same thing. However while psychology helps you understand your life better and uncover why you do the things you do, life coaching is more like your cheerleader along the way, using commonsense tools to guide you forward. Life coaching can be therapeutic, but like other forms of coaching, it isn't therapy. Exhibit 1.3 shows the distinctions that Leonard and others have made between coaching and therapy.

Exhibit 1.3: Differences between coaching and therapy

Coaching is about	Therapy is about
Achievement	Healing
Action	Understanding
Change or transformation	Change
Momentum	Safety
Intuition	Feelings
Joy	Happiness
Performance	Progress
Synchronicity	Timing
Attraction	Protecting
Creating	Resolving

In sum, the primary functions of a life coach are to aid individuals in the achievement of their goals, aims, and aspirations and to help individuals, couples, and groups achieve lasting joy and synchronicity.

Family, couples, and parents coaching

Like all coaching disciplines, family coaching is forward-moving and action-based. It is focused on creating strong family ties and explores ways coachees can deal effectively with issues and flourish as a family "team." Family coaches may be parent coaches or teen coaches (a discipline that is becoming increasingly popular), or they may fall under a variety of other areas of coaching.

As we know, all parents face challenges as they raise their children to adulthood. Parenting involves highs and lows, laughter and joy and excitement, as well as trials, difficulties, and exhaustion. The knowledgeable, objective voice of a parent coach can be helpful and supportive in this parenting process. Parent and family coaching explore innovative and learning-based approaches for raising children, becoming effective parents, and creating healthier, happier families

The focus in couples coaching is on growth, going beyond where the couple is now, and bringing into their life the qualities they want. They may be looking for intimacy and passion harmony increased care and affection clear decisions about contentious topics a shared vision of life together

In couples coaching, the process starts with understanding the couple's hopes, dreams, and aspirations for a love relationship. Then the coach attempts to zoom in on individual aspects of these and create a positive tension for change, which leads to experimentation. Sometimes this involves learning new communication skills, but the principal focus is on using the partners' inner skills to help each see each other and himself or herself through new eyes and to reorient them to what registers as love, enabling their relationship to make a major shift.

1.4 Principal schools of thought in coaching

There are numerous schools of thought in coaching (only some of which I'll present here). The variety and sheer number may seem overwhelming if you're new to the field, but the existence of all these models and theories opens a world of opportunities. They provide an abundance of tools, techniques, methodologies, and models you can put into action. They offer a wealth of information, views, and knowledge that can increase your understanding and hone your ability to think critically and discriminatingly. They may even challenge your assumptions—such as those you may have about the boundary between action and thought—but in rising to these challenges, and in being attentive to your reactions to them, you will become more self-aware and more aware of the people and world around you, more ready to facilitate an effective coaching process.

John Whitmore and the GROW model

The GROW model (or process) is a technique for problem solving or goal setting. It was developed in the U.K. by Sir John Whitmore and his colleagues and used extensively in the corporate coaching market in the late

1980s and 1990s. It was a pioneer model in coaching, and it still has impact today. GROW is very well known in the business arena, but also it has many applications in everyday life. A particular value of GROW is that it provides an effective, structured methodology that simultaneously helps set goals and solve problems. According to Whitmore, it can be used by anyone and does not require special training. It is easy to understand, straightforward, and very thorough. In addition, it can be applied effectively to a variety of issues.

The version of the GROW model in exhibit 1.4 is a modification of Whitmore's original. It ascribes two different meanings to the *O*, for instance, whereas is a bit different from the way Whitmore envisioned it. There are other versions of the model as well, with various views of the stages. (See exhibit 1.5 for a drawing I developed that is closer to the original Whitmore model.)

Exhibit 1.4: A GROW model of coaching

Goal	This is the end point, where the client wants to be. The goal has to be defined in such a way that it is very clear to the client when they have achieved it.
Reality	This is how far the client is away from their goal. If the client were to look at all the steps they need to take in order to achieve the goal, the Reality would be the number of those steps they have completed so far.
Obstacles	There will be Obstacles stopping the client getting from where they are now to where they want to go. If there were no Obstacles the client would already have reached their goal.
Options	Once Obstacles have been identified the client needs to find ways of dealing with them if they are to make progress. These are the Options.
Way Forward	The Options then need to be converted into action steps which will take the client to their goal. These are the Way Forward.

SOURCE: http://en.wikipedia.org/wiki/GROW_model, accessed March 28, 2011.

Like many simple methods, GROW provides users an opportunity to apply a great deal of skill and knowledge at each stage, but the basic process remains the same. There are numerous questions the coach may use at any point, and part of the coach's skill of the coach is knowing which questions to use and how much detail to uncover.

GROW was developed from the Inner Game theory that Timothy Gallwey [17]crafted after noticing that even though he could often see what tennis players were doing incorrectly, simply telling them what they should be doing did not bring about lasting change.

Gallwey's theory is often illustrated by the example of a player who does not keep his or her eye on the ball. To try to correct this, most coaches would give instructions like, "Keep your eye on the ball." The problem with this sort of instruction is that a player would be able to follow it for a short while but would be unable to keep it in the front of his mind in the long term. As a result, progress was slow. Coaches and players grew increasingly frustrated at this laggardly progress, but no one had a better system of coaching. One day, instead of instructing a player to "keep his eye on the ball," Gallwey asked him to say "bounce" out loud when the ball bounced and "hit" when he hit it. The player started to improve without a lot of effort because he was keeping his eye on the ball—without needing to maintain a voice in his head saying, "Keep your eye on the ball." Instead, he was playing a simple game while playing tennis. Once Gallwey saw how play could be improved in this way, he stopped giving generalized instructions and started asking questions that would help players discover for themselves what worked and what needed to change. This was the birth of the Inner Game.

---

[17]   Gallwey, W. T. (1974). *The Inner Game of Tennis* (1st ed.). Random House.

Exhibit 1.5: Whitmore's GROW model of coaching

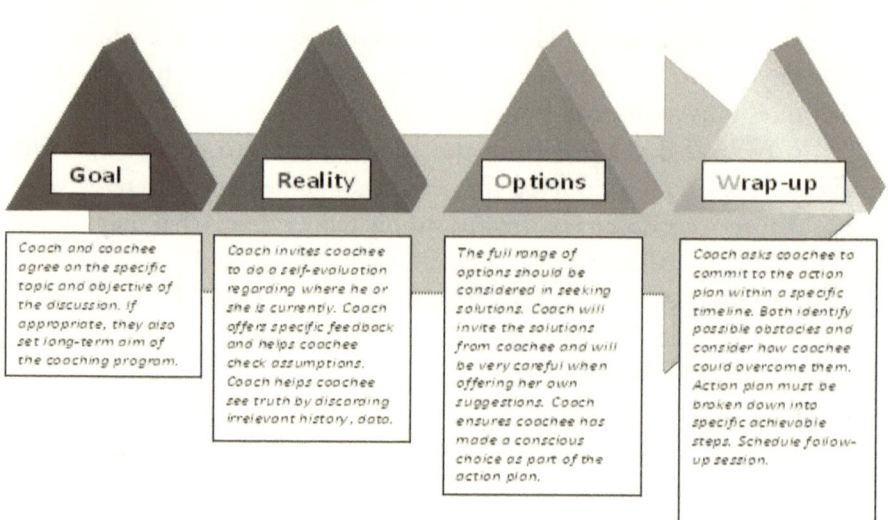

Goal	Reality	Options	Wrap-up
Coach and coachee agree on the specific topic and objective of the discussion. If appropriate, they also set long-term aim of the coaching program.	Coach invites coachee to do a self-evaluation regarding where he or she is currently. Coach offers specific feedback and helps coachee check assumptions. Coach helps coachee see truth by discarding irrelevant history, data.	The full range of options should be considered in seeking solutions. Coach will invite the solutions from coachee and will be very careful when offering her own suggestions. Coach ensures coachee has made a conscious choice as part of the action plan.	Coach asks coachee to commit to the action timeline. Both identify possible obstacles and consider how coachee could overcome them. Action plan must be broken down into specific achievable steps. Schedule follow-up session.

A useful analogy to the GROW model is the plan you might make for an important journey. First, you start with a map; with this, you help your team members decide where they are going (their Goal) and establish where they currently are (their Current Reality). Then you explore various ways of making the journey (the Options). In the final step, establishing the Will, you ensure that your team members are committed to making the journey and prepared for the conditions and obstacles they may meet along the way.

The GROW model is deservedly one of the best known and most widely used coaching models. It provides a simple yet powerful framework for navigating a route through a coaching session and for finding your way when lost.

While GROW is a helpful model/technique, in his later writings, speeches, and conferences, Whitmore insisted that the role of a coach is to help the coachee unlock his or her potential and that this involves more than just using tools such as GROW. The key to unlocking potential is the coach's ability to be aware—that is, the coach must be able to acquire a basic understanding of the organization (or environment) in question, be able to gather facts and information, and be able to determine the relevance of these in light of the organizational dynamics. In addition, because coaching deals with human nature, knowledge of some of the basic tenets of psychology on the part of the coach is important.

One of Whitmore's central precepts is responsibility. An acceptance of responsibility leads to commitment, which optimizes performance. He emphasizes the need to move away from a "blame culture" in which responsibility is constantly shifted onto someone else. According to Whitmore, the job of a manager can be simplified to two central tasks: get the job done and grow the staff. If you apply the principles of coaching to the job, both of those tasks can be accomplished simultaneously.

The GROW model can be used as a self-coaching tool for improving your performance and developing a road map to your personal success. Identify specific goals you wish to achieve; assess your current situation; list your options; make choices (narrow and prioritize your goals); and finally, make steps toward your specific goals and define a time frame.

Before proceeding to the next coaching school of thought, I'd like to offer you two brief ways to use the GROW model. The first is a 3-minute speed-coaching session with a coach and an overweight teenager. The second is a self-coaching exercise.

CBV Reflection ♣ ♠ ♥
Speed Coaching Using the GROW Model

Coach: What area would you like to discuss?

Teenager: I'd like to do some more exercise. (THEME OF COACHING)

Coach: And what would you like out of the coaching session? (QUESTION TO ESTABLISH THE GOAL)

Teenager: I'd like to commit to taking some regular exercise.

Coach: Where are you now when it comes to exercise? (REALITY QUESTION)

Teenager: I'm not exercising as regularly as I'd like.

Coach: So if you'd like to commit to regular exercise (THE GOAL OF THE SESSION), what are your options?

Teenager: I was given a fancy heart-rate wrist monitor; I could learn how to use it. I could get my old bike serviced. I could try a bit of running as well. I could find an event in the future that I could aim for.

Coach: Of all these options, which are you most committed to? (NARROWING DOWN THE OPTIONS)

Teenager: I'd like to use my new heart monitor while I am biking. I was told that I can improve my heart-rate functioning and at the same time reduce my weight. There's a safe 30-km trail in the city that goes around and inside the parks; I think I'd like it.

Coach: So what will you do between now and the next time we talk? (FURTHER NARROWING DOWN TO SPECIFIC OBJECTIVES)

Teenager: I'll call a friend who has similar overweight problem and ask him to join me at least three times a week doing the trail. If he doesn't come with me, I'll do the trail myself. The first time I'll try a 10-km stretch (and watch my heart-rate monitor before and after); the second time I'll bike for 20 km (and also watch my monitor); and the third time I'll try to do the entire 30-km trail (probably during the weekend). I'll also weigh myself today and next week before we meet again.

Coach: Are you sure your objectives are realistic? Will you complete them with or without a friend? (REFLECTIVE QUESTIONS TO ENSURE THE GOALS ARE REALISTIC)

Teenager: I am committed to up to 20 km with or without a friend. Depending on the experience, I may commit to the 30 km alone, but if I find that too difficult, I'll stop at around 20 km.

Coach: OK. I think that I understand your plans and your commitments. I will see you next week, and we will discuss the accomplishments of the objectives and fine-tune your goals. (WRAP-UP)

Teenager: See you next week.

CBV Reflection ♣ ♠ ♥

Self-coaching: Using the GROW model on yourself

Whether you've begun to go through the GROW self-coaching steps I mentioned above and are trying to choose among a few possible goals, or already have a goal in mind, you can use this GROW exercise. Simply choose one goal and ask yourself these four questions:

1. Why?

   _____
   _____
   _____
   _____

2. Why not?

   _____
   _____
   _____
   _____

3. Why not me?

   _____
   _____
   _____
   _____

4. Why not now?

   _____
   _____
   _____
   _____

The Co-Active Coaching model

The central principle of Co-Active Coaching, developed by Laura Whitworth and colleagues,[18] is that both parties actively collaborate in the coaching partnership. It is based on the following four fundamental principles:

- the client is naturally resourceful and capable of finding the answers to her challenges herself

- the agenda comes from the client and is the key focus of the coaching relationship

- the coaching addresses the client as a whole person

- the coaching relationship is a "designed alliance" for promoting action and learning, in which the client, and not the coach, is ultimately in control

This model concentrates on the development of specific coaching skills and techniques rather than on the content or structure of a coaching session.

The purpose of the Co-Active Coach is to meet clients' needs and help them achieve the results they want. The client's agenda is at the very center of this model. Whitworth and her colleagues highlight three important elements of this:

- fulfillment (achieving success and reaching client's full potential)

- balance (addressing all aspects of the client's life)

- process (focusing on the means as well as the end result)

Based on the above, the authors propose five key coaching skills: listening, intuition, curiosity, action-learning, and self-management. The Co-Active Coaching model is graphically represented in exhibit 1.6.

---

[18] Whitworth, L., Kimsey-house, H., Kimsey-house, K. K., & Sandahl, P. (2007). *Co-Active Coaching: New Skills for Coaching People Toward Success in Work and Life* (2nd ed.). Davis Black.

Exhibit 1.6: The Co-Active Coaching model

SOURCE: Adapted from Donnan, S. (2007, May). Appreciative Inquiry and Co-Active Coaching. *AI Practitioner*. p. 37.

An inquiry, which is the base of the Co-Active Coaching, is a powerful question that is not meant to be answered immediately, but instead, offers the coachee an opportunity for reflection, discovery, and learning. The power questions, or inquiries, below were adapted from *Co-Active Coaching*, by Whitworth, Kimsey-house, Kimsey-house, and Sandahl.

CBV Reflection ♣ ♠ ♥

Sample Co-Active Coaching Power Questions

- What do I want?
- What am I tolerating?
- Where am I not being realistic/practical?
- Where is my attention?
- What is the difference between a wish and a goal?
- If my whole attention is focused on producing the result, what will I have to give up?

- What is working for me?

- What will it take to keep me on track?

- What am I willing/unwilling to change?

- What am I settling for?

- What is it to be creative/passionate/focused/a leader?

- What is it to speak/act from my heart?

- What does it mean to be proactive/centered/optimistic?

- What is present when I am at my best?

- What motivates me?

- What am I resisting?

- If I were at my best, what would I do right now?

- What are my assumptions (about life, work, family, etc.)?

- Where do I limit myself?

- Where do I hold back?

- What are my expectations for this project (or life, family, work—area under consideration)?

- How can I make this easy?

- Who can I get to play with me on this project?

- What have I learned about myself (by contemplating these questions and throughout the project)?

Advocates of Co-Active Coaching describe the process as "a thought clarification process." Two of its underlying assumptions distinguish it from other coaching schools of thought. The first is that no other person can ever know enough about you to decide for you more effectively than you can decide for yourself. Based on this assumption, most people's primary need is not the advice or direction of others; it is clarifying one's own thinking. So the Co-Active Coaching process facilitates your clarifying your own thinking. Co-Active Coaching's second underlying assumption is that people are intrinsically creative, resourceful, and whole. Coaching is a way to for you to discover, with the aid of a trained coach, what you value, what you need, and what you want out of your life.

This form of coaching is called "co-active" because it is a customized designed alliance between coach and client to maximize the benefit of coaching to each client. A good historical example of co-active coaching is that of Socrates. Whenever a student came to him with a question, he would "answer" with a question—and continue doing this until, eventually, the student discovered the answer himself.

The Neuro-Linguistic Programming (NLP) coaching method [19]

Neuro-linguistic programming as a study of human functioning has, since its inception in the early 1970s, permeated virtually every field of human endeavor, particularly with relation to communication, influence, and change in the business world. Dr. John Grinder, co-originator of NLP with Dr. Richard Bandler, describes NLP most simply as "the modeling of excellent behavior/genius."

Historical background

According to Grinder, Bandler, and their colleague Frank Pucelik had been having fun mimicking the behavior of recently deceased Fritz Perls (the cofounder of the Gestalt school of thought in psychology) in evening Gestalt classes with students when they noticed that they and the students were achieving remarkable therapeutic results by playing at "being" Fritz Perls. Thinking that Perls's use of language, among other things, might be at the center of their apparent success, Bandler invited Grinder, who was an

---

[19] **IMPORTANT NOTE:** The basics of this model have been described in a series of books including *Frogs into Princes* (Bandler & Grinder, 1979), *Neuro-Linguistic Programming Vol. I* (Dilts, Grinder, Bandler, & DeLozier, 1980), *Reframing* (Bandler & Grinder, 1982), *Using Your Brain* (Bandler, 1985), Turtles All the Way Down (DeLozier & Grinder, 1995), and *Whispering in the Wind* (Bostic & Grinder, 2001). Following several exchanges with John Grinder, he graciously agreed to have the section written by his colleagues. **More than 95% of this section is an original contribution by Bill Phillips and Alessandro de Vita Zublena** of AdZ Conseil Coaching for Leaders, based in Lausanne, Switzerland (www.adzconseil.com). Phillips and Zublena are members of The International Trainers Academy of NLP and work in close association with John Grinder and Carmen Bostic St Clair.

assistant professor of linguistics at the University of California, Santa Cruz, to sit in on the classes and help them make sense of what was happening.

Grinder decided that because Bandler and Pucelik had modeled Perls by pure mimicry without understanding what they were doing, he would model them in the same way by running parallel classes with other students until he could reproduce their results. Bandler and he then stepped back to analyze the process, identifying and encoding the patterns of behavior and language use that seemed to yield these results. They taught these encoded patterns to others and noticed that their model enabled naïve subjects consistently to reproduce Perls's unique talent.

At about this time, Bandler assisted at a workshop delivered by Virginia Satir, a leading family therapist considered a genius in her field. Bandler noticed that she employed a number of questions and language patterns that were almost identical to those of Perls, and she agreed to allow Bandler and Grinder to model her work over a period of months. This modeling work, and the addition of language patterns inspired by Noam Chomsky's pioneering work in transformational grammar, led to their development of the meta-model for language and its publication in their 1975 book *The Structure of Magic*.

They were later introduced to the psychiatrist Milton Erickson by Gregory Bateson. Bateson was so impressed by their modeling process that he thought at last someone might be able to reveal the secrets of Erickson's genius with hypnosis and trances—after many prominent specialists he had sent to study Erickson over the years had failed. Based on their encoding of Erickson's very unusual language and nonverbal behavior, and in particular what he revealed about workings of the unconscious, they presented to the world a new, explicit, and teachable model not only of genius and its practical acquisition but of the interplay of human neurology, language, and behavioral functioning (programming). A series of new discoveries followed from these observations as Grinder and Bandler coded and published descriptions of their experiences. Here are two of these discoveries:

- the matching of people's unconscious choice of predicates to thinking modes (seeing, hearing, and feeling) and the cues offered by corresponding eye movements

- the structuring of memories in the characteristics of internal pictures, sound, and sensation (submodalities) and the ways that these modes of cognition not only were implicated in the structure of clients' difficulties, but could be manipulated in ways that helped clients to "reprogram" themselves to achieve more desired and healthy responses

The patterns that Grinder and Bandler encoded were originally intended to be therapy, and at the core of these originally therapeutically directed procedures and patterns are modes of calibrating unconscious physiological responses, establishing and maintaining rapport, and leading clients' attention so they can achieve more choice (see footnote 15 for more on calibration). These include communication skills that have since become ubiquitous, such as matching and mirroring and the use of "specifying" and "influencing language." NLP experts claim that such skills were not explicitly available before they were modeled and coded by Grinder and Bandler. They suggest that practitioners of NLP, rather than learning fixed sets of useful questions to ask, learn to recognize the underlying syntactic structures of the client's language and to apply these patterns of language to constructing questions and challenges based on what that specific client has just said or done.

The purpose of their original meta-model, they say, was not to help the coach (or therapist) gather information or understanding, but rather to help the client expand his or her restricted model of the world and from that develop a set of possible solutions. This gives a very different meaning to accessing inner resources from those implied in other coaching methods, in which the client is guided to formulate her or his own solutions.

The discovery of mirror neurons

The now-ubiquitous matching and mirroring mentioned above were patterns of functioning detected and explicated by Bandler and Grinder in the early 1970s. They were at the heart of their modeling process, which leads to the unconscious uptake of excellent performance, and were proposed as effective ways to achieve significant relationships of rapport. In the mid-1990s, researchers in neuroscience[20] discovered what

---

[20]   Rizzolatti first published his findings in 1996, but later summarized and updated his research in Rizzolatti, G. (2005). The mirror neuron system and its function in humans. *Anatomy and Embryology*, 210(5–6), 419–421.

are now called "mirror neurons." These are apparently the neurological mechanisms responsible for what Grinder and Bandler had observed and coded twenty years earlier.

The finding of mirror neurons was hailed by world-renowned neuroscientist V. S. Ramachandran in 2000 as the single most important unpublicized story of the decade. He believes that "mirror neurons will do for psychology what DNA did for biology."[21] Mirror neurons were first discovered in monkeys and are now known to exist in humans, in much more complex configurations and with more highly sophisticated capacities.[22] Grinder claims, "It seems inevitable that our work in NLP discovering/creating patterning that works (using direct experience and calibration primarily) will continue to run some decades in advance of the discovery of the underlying mechanisms that are the neurological correlates. How is that possible? We simply experiment and use consequences and calibration[23] as tools to guide us."

The New Code of NLP

Grinder and Bandler parted company at the end of the 1970s. After this, Grinder recognized what he considers a series of "flaws" in their original encoding. Apart from noticing that several patterns could be reduced and

---

[21]   Ramachandran, V. S. (2000, May). Mirror neurons and imitation learning as the driving force behind "the great leap forward" in human evolution. *Edge, 69*, 29. http://www.edge.org/3rd_culture/ramachandran/ramachandran_p1.html.

[22]   Rizzolatti, G., Craighero, L. (2004). The mirror neuron system. *Annual Rev Neurosci 27*, 169–192.

[23]   *Calibration*, as the term is used in NLP, is an acute attention to all of a client's conscious and unconscious responses, from changes in voice tone, skin color, blinking, and breathing to choice of words and many more. Because tracking so many details is impossible for the conscious mind, NLP practitioners are trained to allow their peripheral vision and hearing to collect movements and changes, and to respond as if "intuitively" to what others say and do. This is a very specific kind of attention-giving. New Code practitioners are even more highly trained in this, they say, because they work largely content-free, so seeing and hearing is sometimes all they have to guide them. If the coach's calibration is faulty, his or her competence is automatically impaired.

made more elegant, he realized that the amount of information gathering (verbal eliciting of internal processes, values, and beliefs) in the original encoding

1. created the problem of the coach's being obliged to interpret meaning via his or her own internal representations, due to lack of precision inherent in the semantic functioning of words

2. meant the client had to reveal the content of sometimes deeply private experiences (failing to respect the client's absolute confidentiality)

3. demanded mostly processing and behavior change from the client's conscious attention, when it was obvious from experience that changes were both accepted or generated and subsequently executed by unconscious processes

The use of terms such as *conscious* and *unconscious* is considered metaphorical in NLP, in the sense that a separate "mind" in a body is not a tangible neurological function (Descarte's error). This can be imagined as a continuum of attention from that which is immediately noticeable to that which lies outside immediate attention, such as the sensation of toes on the reader's left foot right now or examples of subtle changes in the appearance of an individual as she processes her experiences (e.g. elements of mirroring, breathing, gestures noted in rapport building). Adherents of NLP describe the further reaches of the continuum of unconscious as the total functioning of autonomic and endocrine systems, body chemistry, metabolism, and the like being conducted on "automatic pilot" and normally outside conscious manipulation.

In their book *Whispering in the Wind*, Carmen Bostic St Clair and Grinder suggest that learning how to create a "partnership" with the unconscious allows the use of *yes* and *no* signaling systems (involuntarily felt physiological changes in the body) to access new choices of response to challenging and unpredictable circumstances.[24] These signals tend to elicit a "wow!" response from individuals when they first encounter them.

---

[24] Bostic St Clair, C., & Grinder, J. (2001). *Whispering in the Wind*. J&C Enterprises. p. 218.

Gregory Bateson said that the logic of unconscious process is profoundly different from the logic of conscious process, and the collision of these two processes is the basis of creativity and art.

Grinder further observed that many of the people he and Bandler had trained often worked effectively with clients but demonstrated little evidence of having worked on themselves. He now insists that congruency within the coach is a prerequisite for high-quality, respectful, and effective change-work.

These observations prompted him to re-code many of the original patterns and to supersede a number of them with the designed (rather than modeled) processes of the New Code. What most people in the world know as NLP is what the New Code people now call the "Classic Code" of NLP. With Bostic, Grinder has continued to develop and elaborate procedures that assign choice and execution of change to the client's unconscious. Rather than changes of behavior, or of beliefs and values, New Code processes are directed at choice of and access to physiological "states." Beliefs and ineffective behaviors need not be directly addressed but are simply handled through the use of the high performance states generated by New Code games and activities. These high performance states are then associated with the context selected by the client.

New Code Change Format in action

Example one, general manager of a banking group:

A General Manager of a banking group had a fear of giving performance feedback to a colleague. As he prepared for a meeting, he would perspire, experience stomach cramps and find it difficult to breathe because of pressure in his chest. During the meeting, he would struggle with discussing performance improvements, because his colleague was a sensitive person and the GM was afraid of hurting him. After his coach took him through the New Code Change Format, playing "The Alphabet Game," the GM confessed he was skeptical that this could help him.

After the next meeting with his colleague, however, the GM reported that during the meeting he became aware he had not experienced his usual symptoms while preparing for it. He also noticed he was hearing himself speak in a relaxed, informal way, even using language and expressions not typical of him. No sweating, no cramps, no sign of labored breathing. In addition, his colleague noted how different he seemed and how much he had enjoyed and found useful their feedback discussion.

The General Manager reported how deeply surprised and gratified he was that such a big change could be achieved in just one game.

Example two, a motorbike racer:

A well-known motorbike racer had a problem when faced with fleeting opportunities to overtake a rider in the narrow space on the inside of bends on the racetrack. Despite all his efforts to overcome his hesitation at making this complex and dangerous maneuver, he continued to unconsciously brake at the critical moment. When coached through the New Code Change Format, he expressed disbelief that a simple game could possibly help him.

During his next race, he passed the then-leading rider in the race on the inside of a tight bend without braking and improved his own position in the race, coming in third. He reported his amazement, adding that at the moment of overtaking, he had no conscious perception of what he was doing. He only became aware of it as he came out of the bend.

Coaching with New Code NLP

Bill Phillips and Alessandro de Vita Zublena

For NLP coaches, all learning in the context of coaching is experiential. What is important is noticing what works, and giving freedom and choice to their clients in contexts where they normally have no choice or choices which are not satisfactory to the client. The coach's purpose is to elicit, define, refine, challenge, and facilitate the client's expression of goals and intentions. This is contained in a process that includes gaining rapport, establishing frames and contracting, eliciting information, creating action plans, getting commitment, and following up. Understanding the problem is not an essential element in the successful change process. In fact, it can be quite dangerous for the coach to attempt to understand a client's problem because it can lead

---

to projection, misunderstanding, and especially unethical practices of imposing the coach's own perception, beliefs, and values on the client.

The problem is not the problem. The problem is the state in which the client approaches the context in which the problem resides. So what is needed in order to jump into a successful change process? There is absolutely no need for content about the problem. Instead, explicit and precise information about the context and a set of manipulations, in the most positive and ethical sense, are required to create a high performance state in the client, and to ensure that when a client next enters the context in which the problem exists, he or she innovates from a high performance state.

The New Code approach to coaching emphasizes the importance of state over behavior change (this is illustrated below). Clients are helped to experience and identify sensory evidence of achieving their intentions through a structured guidance process. This allows a contract to be made between the coach and the client, and facilitates subsequent evaluation of results, especially with corporate clients, regarding specific objectives and outcomes.

The New Code Change Format is a powerful, simple, and effective way to help a client create "generative change" in a particular class of circumstances. Four key steps are

1. The client identifies a context or situation that he or she wishes to experience differently and is helped to "see and hear" representations of himself, performing as he currently would in this chosen situation. The client imagines this as if he were watching himself on film just a few feet away.

2. Once the client reports an adequate representation both verbally and nonverbally (the latter verified through calibration by the coach), he steps into and experiences directly "being in" the representation without attempting to change anything. When effective, a clear shift in physiology is observed (calibrated) by the coach. This is the physiology of the client's present state.

3. After the client steps away from the spot and shakes off its related physiological sensations, the coach guides him through a New Code game designed to produce a shift in state that will enable the client to respond in a new and effective way in the given context through

the development of a high performance state. The effect of playing the game is that the client reaches a point where he stop trying to correct little faults and enters what might be termed a state of "flow" (similar to an athlete's being "in the zone").

4. When the client begins to exhibit this "zone" or "flow" physiology, identified by the coach, the client is invited to step immediately back into his original imaged context. What the coach expects to calibrate now is that this new state becomes associated with the context in which the client wanted a difference. The coach is also verifying that there is no trace of the original physiology associated with the client's former state. There is no discussion or analysis with the client of the new experience because that can undermine success through conscious interference and limit the generalization of the new choices in the client's experience. The net effect is that the next time the client experiences the context, instead of his old reaction, some new and more appropriate responses will arise borne out of an unconscious recognition of the surroundings and an immediate and an immediate and unconscious reactivation of the high performance state.

The unrehearsed and effective result of this format gives meaning to the term *generative change*. The specific shift in state is unconsciously prompted and gives rise to not only appropriate choices, but often quite novel and surprising ones (see "New Code Formation in Action" examples in this chapter). Such responses cannot be rehearsed because the specific events in the given context inevitably are unpredictable. The key word is *appropriate*.

When a person has only one way to respond in a given context, he or she could well be characterized as an unhappy robot. If with the help of her coach, she examines possibilities and rehearses new skills or behaviors, then as long as the expected happens (almost never), she may be said to be a happy robot; she has access to more than one reaction. The weakness of this approach shows up when the unexpected, the unpredictable, happens. The client cannot find an adequate response because she has rehearsed only behavioral change. The spontaneous creation of an appropriate response in the face of the unexpected is evidence of generative change. The client's system has learned how to learn. This was achieved by working with states rather than with behaviors or beliefs and values and is a key differentiator for coaching with New Code NLP.

According to New Code NLP specialists, changes in state can and do alter what is attended to (perceived, the movement of attention) and thus give rise to altered internal "models of the world" and the choices implied by such a radical shift. They insist that their purpose is not to teach an unhappy robot how to become a happy robot. Their goal is to create a person who, on the spot, on his or her feet, can generate creative and successful behavior from a high performance state without needing to know at any point what specific behavior will occur.

The New Code Change Format Phillips and Zublena describe in "Coaching with New Code NLP" is just one of many procedures NLP coaches employ to assist coachees with changing states. A key characteristic it shares with most other New Code processes is an emphasis on the coach's functioning content-free. Here, a question immediately presents itself: How does the coach know what is going on if the only information available is likely to be changes in the client's appearance? New Code coaches and practitioners are, they say, trained to refine their skills in calibrating—skills such as differentiating between the conscious and unconscious external cues—beyond those normally developed in Classic Code NLP.[25]

Yet most coaches know that clients will frequently insist on telling their story and want their coaches to show they can, and do, listen. The attention of a New Code coach, however, is said to be on detecting the patterns, tonal emphases, and indicators of how a client constructs his or her inner reality and not on understanding the content and meaning of the story. The New Code term for this is "listening off the top." Staying with the process of their clients' experiences is the most respectful way to assist them, allowing coaches to avoid imposing their own perceptual filters, values, and beliefs.

In addition, they believe that those working as coaches who fail to make the distinction between process and content are quite dangerous. They are dangerous, New Code advocates say, because without a clear operational appreciation of the process/content distinction, coaches will, even with the best of intentions, impose their own perceptions, beliefs,

---

[25]   For more on New Code training, go to www.itanlp.com.

and values on their clients without even realizing what they are doing. This makes them doubly dangerous: They are imposing, and yet are totally unaware of it.

Some New Code core principles

In Part III, chapter 2 of *Whispering in the Wind* (p. 317), Bostic and Grinder explain the distinction they make between first and second order change. The New Code NLP Coach selects interventions based on these principles. If the client has goals to change addictions, physical symptoms, or behaviors with significant secondary gains or payoffs, the coach will select processes working with the (usually) unconsciously held intention of the unwanted experiences (second order processes). Clients' unconscious responses to these interventions are always bounded by the requirement that they satisfy the intention, making them appropriate and ecological, and more likely to be lasting changes. Many of the Classic Code processes that function at the first order of change, such as anchoring techniques, have been prone to reversion over time.

However all NLP patterns, both New and Classic Code, share certain essential qualities:

> All patterns and formats in NLP (Classic and New Code) are nothing more than instructions to the agent of change where to fix his/her attention and where to direct the attention of the client. The NLP Coach has a clear representation of patterning in the change work, e.g. a description of the pattern, the consequences of the use of the pattern and the selection criteria, meaning the identification of the conditions or contexts in which the selection and application of the pattern is appropriate. (*Whispering in the Wind*, p. 314)

A further key feature of the NLP coach's approach, modeled originally from Milton Erickson is tasking. In this, the client is given homework designed to provide counter examples of limiting behaviors or convictions. In one light-hearted example, Grinder tasked a young man who had difficulty approaching relationships with women to conduct what appeared to be a legitimate and serious marketing survey in a high-class women's underwear store. Grinder set this up in agreement with the store and a manufacturing supplier. It resulted not only in a successful survey but more important, in the client's happy report of dates with two different women.

Guiding their clients to self-sufficiency and independence through the accessing of high performance states and discovering and exercising the ability to induce change within themselves (i.e., the clients) are core principles for New Code NLP coaches. Bostic and Grinder assert that when a coach successfully, consistently, and reliably practices self-application of NLP patterning, he or she knows the difference between process and content and is therefore able to recognize and use the multitude of unconscious signals that clients offer. Coaches do not become archaeological investigators of the past, focusing attention on what happened in the past and how to go from there to the future the client wishes for; rather they know how to elicit a context and generate a state in which the client becomes competent and independent. For these coaches, the change process is never finished; each successful change opens a door to a new set of possibilities. Coaches working with the New Code of NLP continue to experiment, to learn, and to develop further patterning in the art of coaching.

A final note about NLP

Although the bulk of the section on NLP was written by current colleagues of John Grinder's (i.e., Bill Phillips and Alessandro de Vita Zublena), it is important to mention the work Richard Bandler has done in this field since he and Grinder parted ways. Bandler has developed new processes deriving from the original NLP, most notably, Design Human Engineering (DHE) and Neuro-Hypnotic Repatterning (NHR). Both methods employ a variety of communication and persuasion skills and use self-hypnosis to excite motivation produce change. Like all his work, they are about personal freedom. The common denominator is communication. As Bandler put it, "Language is communication and it is all hypnosis; this is how language works."

When creating NHR, he wanted to get people out of the "personal jails" they build for themselves so they could have greater freedom. He observed that people were not having enough fun. It is not that people are not capable of it; they are just not using their neurology in a way that produces pleasure. Neuro-Hypnotic Repatterning uses very deep trance tools to make very pervasive changes across a wide range of behaviors and teaches people to spend more time practicing feeling good than feeling bad. NHR takes people beyond communication skills and beyond persuasion and enables them to use their brain chemistry and neurology to bring about changes in beliefs, thoughts, and feelings. According to Bandler, NHR moves people swiftly, painlessly, and with laughter into better ways of being.

NHR uses the hypnotic process to restructure experiences that people have at the neurological and chemical level. Instead of teaching people to lead with their minds, NHR teaches them to lead with their feelings. They learn to saturate their neurology with the chemicals that make them feel good. Bandler insists that "if you get your whole body in the right state," you can do almost anything. NHR helps a client get her body to this state, by enabling her to redesign the way she connects with herself—physically, mentally, and to some extent, spiritually. NHR makes changes using some principles from time, memory processing, feelings, and language.

Even though Bandler and Grindler stopped collaborating decades ago, they both still work in the field they co-founded, albeit with marked differences in how each evolves that field. NHR and DHE are Bandler's rightful applications of NLP. Bandler continues to refine and develop competence in the way the nervous system stores and processes experience and memories in the subcomponents of seeing, hearing, and feeling, referred to as "submodalities," and to manipulate (in the most positive sense) those mechanisms through trance and hypnosis to help clients have more choice.

Grinder and Bostic have gone back to much of the original encoding and patterning of NLP, and refined, simplified, or re-coded the way NLP change-work is done. They give much greater importance to congruence in the practitioner, to respecting clients' privacy by not engaging in exploration of reasons and meanings, and to working with clients' unconscious reactions, observed through heightened calibration of signals that are beyond clients' awareness. Their work is based on the concept that the deepest changes are effected by satisfying unconsciously held intentions rather than by manipulating behavioral outputs.

Emotional intelligence as a coaching tool

Emotional intelligence (EI) comprises all the non-IQ areas of human intelligence. Often called people skills, street smarts, common sense, or savvy, this wide array of capabilities is emerging as the most important set of competencies in business. These personal and social, managerial and leadership skills are increasingly recognized as the core of what separates star performers from the rest of the pack.

Peter Salovey of Yale and John D. Mayer of the University of New Hampshire defined the term *emotional intelligence* in a groundbreaking 1990 article in the journal *Imagination, Cognition, and Personality* as "the subset of social intelligence that involves *the ability to monitor one's own and others' feelings and emotions, to discriminate among them, and to use this information to guide one's thinking and actions.*" Since then, many have researched EI and written about what it is, how it works, and what people can do to improve one's EQ (the measurement of one's EI; often the terms are used interchangeably). This has had an important impact on the coaching profession, with Daniel Goleman's 1995 book *Emotional Intelligence: Why It Can Matter More Than IQ* having become essential reading. Many coaches incorporate EI concepts, techniques, and tools into their work.

Emotional intelligence is, in fact, relevant to all of us, because it encompasses the most important skills we use every day, skills that determine how well we know ourselves, how well we deal with everything that happens to us, and how well we deal with others. And whether we know it or not, these skills are vital to our success.

The available evidence shows that an individual cannot achieve extraordinary levels of success without a high level of competency in the core EI areas (see exhibit 1.7 for core EI competencies). The professional landscape is littered with bright, would-be leaders with great technical skills who failed because of their lack of self-knowledge, self-control, or confidence or their inability to understand others and build trusting, empowering, mutually beneficial, and productive relationships with their constituents.[26]

---

[26] Boyatzis, R., & McKee, A. (2005). *Resonant Leadership: Renewing Yourself and Connecting with Others Through Mindfulness, Hope, and Compassion.* Harvard Business Press.

Practicing (or being coached) to increase emotional intelligence, an individual needs

- to know oneself by enhancing emotional literacy and recognizing patterns

- choose oneself by applying consequential thinking, navigating emotions, engaging intrinsic motivation, and exercising optimism

- give oneself by increasing empathy and pursuing noble goals

Some people can practice EI without a coach, but for others a coach can be instrumental. A coach can be an objective observer who can help clients focus on their fundamental beliefs and assessments, change their behavior, and improve their decision making in those aspects of EI where they are most deficient.

Exhibit 1.7: Emotional intelligence competencies

At ESADE (the business school where I've taught since 2002), we use a LEAD program with all MBA students.[27] Their EI competencies are assessed, and they are assigned a coach for the duration of the program. I have seen individuals make tremendous progress improving their EQs when working with a coach. Emotional intelligence is combining the head and the heart, and a coach can help make the combination work. The LEAD program at ESADE plays a critical role in the school's ranking as one of the top 10 MBA programs in the world.

However, EI as a method and model of coaching can be problematic, and I'd advise you to do more homework before venturing into this area—whether you are looking for a coach who claims to be an expert in this field or you are simply looking for an EI tool or method to incorporate into your work or life. Many of the mass-marketed "emotional intelligence" training courses discuss "self-awareness," "resilience," and "authenticity" under the heading "emotional skills." Clearly these concepts are not emotions. They are personality characteristics that may or may not have an impact on how an individual deals with his or her emotions.

Because coaching works in the domain of emotions, it is imperative that all coaches have clear definitions of emotions and clear boundaries when working with them. Coaches who work with EI must know what constitutes negative and positive emotional states, be able to distinguish between the two, and possess a finely honed understanding of which aspects of emotions a coach can work with effectively. Naturally, coaches who do not have a background in the behavioral sciences are hesitant, sometimes apprehensive, about working with a coachee's emotions.

---

[27] The LEAD Program in ESADE was developed by Daniel Goleman and Richard Boyatzis and adapted for use in Europe by ESADE. It is a series of practical and personal exercises carried out via an online platform and individual coaching sessions. Based on his or her ideal leadership profile, each student crafts a personal development strategy that continues beyond ESADE. These strategies have a direct impact on the students' development as executives.

CBV Reflection ♣ ♠ ♥

Emotional Intelligence Quiz*

Complete this if you are in a management position and responsible for others in your organization.

Circle the Yes or No for each statement. Think of your usual behavior, not the occasional exceptions. Be very honest in your responses.

1. I am aware of how I respond in crisis situations.	Yes	No
2. My workplace behavior is consistent with my core values.	Yes	No
3. I have examined and am clear about my core values.	Yes	No
4. I can articulate my core values with my staff, colleagues and bosses.	Yes	No
5. My management style is flexible enough to be functional.	Yes	No
6. I am proud of the way I handle myself with the most difficult staff.	Yes	No
7. I clearly communicate my ideas to the highest levels of management.	Yes	No
8. I consciously draw from many different leadership styles and approaches, based on the situation.	Yes	No
9. I understand the different drivers, both personal and professional, that dictate my staff's actions.	Yes	No
10. My approach to motivation is highly individualized, based on the unique needs of the individual.	Yes	No
11. I am clear about how politics impact activity in this organization.	Yes	No
12. I know my staff's strengths and weaknesses.	Yes	No
13. I find ways to maneuver around obstacles.	Yes	No
14. My successes are not achieved in isolation; they are the result of concerted, coordinated, collaborative activities.	Yes	No
15. I encourage my staff to communicate with and assist other departments.	Yes	No
16. I regularly reach out for help from my peers.	Yes	No

Each of these statements corresponds to a competency in one of the first four quadrants in exhibit 1.7. Total the number of Yes answers for each statement:

Self-awareness	Questions 1, 2, 3, 4	_____
Self-management	Questions 5, 6, 7, 8	_____
Social awareness	Questions 9, 10, 11, 12	_____
Relationship management	Questions 13, 14, 15, 16	_____

After analyzing your answers, assess yourself and look for developmental opportunities. Alone or with a help of a coach, you can plot a course for growth based on building or strengthening your competencies in a selected area or areas.

*NOTE: This quiz has been developed for demonstration only; it has not been tested or validated. Also it is an exercise in progress and does not yet test competencies in all five quadrants of exhibit 1.7.

Trust, Reading People, and Emotional Intelligence

David Caruso

Michael was an executive coaching client who worked for the NYC office of a major Japanese investment bank. The head of HR referred Michael for coaching citing fairly vague issues, such as Michael "did not play office politics well." As a result, his managerial duties were removed, and he returned to the trading desk full time. At the same time, he was thought to be very skilled and the bank did not want to lose him to a competitor, so the VP of this group asked HR what could be done to help Michael.

As part of the executive coaching process, Michael took several assessments, along with an ability-based measure of emotional intelligence, the Mayer, Salovey, Caruso Emotional Intelligence Test (MSCEIT). Personality self-assessment revealed that Michael viewed himself as a good "people person," with excellent social skills and the ability to read others.

However, his results on the MSCEIT suggested otherwise. The MSCEIT measures a person's actual emotional intelligence abilities in an objective manner rather than relying upon a person's self-view. Michael scored in the high end of Competent on the MSCEIT. However, his Scatter Score was 116, suggesting that his Total score might not be a good estimate of his overall EI. (MSCEIT standard scores are similar to IQ scores with a mean of 100 and standard deviation of 15.) Therefore, we needed to examine his ability and task scores. His lowest score, in the Improve range, was for Perceiving Emotions, an ability measured by correctly guessing the emotions expressed by faces and pictures. He was expert at Understanding the causes of emotions, skilled at Using emotions to aid in thinking and connecting emotionally with others, and competent at Managing his own and others' emotions.

I discussed the MSCEIT with Michael, wondering whether he misread the instructions, and clearly he had not. So his score on Perceiving Emotions could be valid. I asked some questions in the MSCEIT Feedback Guide to explore this issue. Michael said he felt very uncomfortable making judgments about people and their emotions noting: "I really don't know how the person feels"; "it is possible that the person with a bit of a frown was not sad, but who am I to say?"

He really did not want to be judgmental about people, and given his inclination to see the best in others, rarely "saw" negative emotions in others. This issue around being too positive was reflected by a high Emotion Bias Score, which measures the test taker's propensity to endorse more negative or positive emotions in test stimuli.

Given his ability to empathize with others (Use emotions) and understand the causes of emotions (Understand), we leveraged his analytical ability to teach him to better read people. First, I had him focus on his own feelings (using a simple two-dimensional graph we call the Mood Meter) and then label the feelings using his extensive emotion vocabulary. Next, I used pictures of emotions to teach him the basic expressions. We watched videos without the sound to guess how people felt. We observed people around the office. He saw this as a puzzle to be solved, which appealed to his keen intellect. We talked about looking for a mismatch between what people say and how they say it—that is, that how a person feels about an idea, trade, or meeting will be revealed more by his or her tone and face than by his or her words. We discussed his high Bias score, and I told him that although he thought he was not imposing himself on others, he actually was imposing a positive bias on his emotional perceptions. This caught his attention.

However, all this work got him only so far, so I encouraged a simple remedial strategy: to ask people, "How are you?" and to get specific when doing so, by asking, for example, "Are you OK with the direction of this project?"; "Are you completely satisfied with the meeting?" and so forth. It was a great strategy and worked well for Michael. He may not have increased his actual emotional intelligence; in fact, little is known about how malleable such an intelligence is. However, he developed some greater knowledge and more important, critical remedial or compensatory strategies (such as confirming his initial perceptions with others as appropriate).

Michael's management responsibilities were eventually returned to him. Apparently, his poor "political skills" were really his difficulties reading people and not attending to subtle emotional cues.

David R. Caruso co-wrote The Emotionally Intelligent Manager, a practical, how-to book on emotional intelligence, with Peter Salovey. David also helped to develop the Mayer, Salovey, Caruso Emotional Intelligence Test (disclosure: Caruso receives royalties from the sale of the MSCEIT). He conducts training, research, and consulting on emotional intelligence. E-mail: david@eiskills.com.

Appreciative Inquiry (AI) coaching: concept and methodology

David Cooperrider and Suresh Srivastva developed Appreciative Inquiry (often known as AI) in the 1980s as a variation of action research. This theory contends that organizations, and other systems, do not present a problem to be solved but a miracle to be embraced. An organization that looks for problems will keep finding them, and an organization that appreciates what is best in itself will discover more and more that is good. From these discoveries, it can build a new future in which the best becomes more common. AI uses a particular way of asking questions and envisioning the future that fosters positive relationships and goodness in a person, a situation, or an organization and that enhances a system's capacity for collaboration and change. AI's four-process cycle consists of discover, dream, design, and destiny (or deliver).[28]

Appreciative Inquiry (AI) is also distinct from other coaching schools of thought in the emphasis it puts on the system. It has been defined as the study of what gives life to human systems when they are at their best. Its advocates describe the AI coaching process as a "co-creative partnership" between the client, the coach, and the relevant social system (e.g., organization, team, family). Often the process is used with a group within a system, such as a team in an organization or several members of a family, but it can be used with an individual.

So Appreciative Inquiry is both a specific methodology and a perspective. To further understand this, we need only look at the two words that make it up:

- *Appreciative* has two meanings: to look for the best/acknowledge the best (in something) and to increase (something) in value, such as when a stock or real estate appreciates;

- *Inquiry* means to seek understanding using a process based on provocative questions.

In an AI coaching session, the coach asks provocative questions to draw out powerful success stories and identify the factors that are already working well within a human system. This understanding becomes the basis for helping the clients bring into being what they want more of (which is dramatically different from the usual cultural focus on reducing what they want less of).

The specific methodology of Appreciative Inquiry provides the tools to do this, involving both left and right brains and exploring the past, present and future. It consists of five main phases (the four-process cycle mentioned earlier and an introductory interview):

- **Affirmative Topic Choice:** The coach conducts an interview using several provocative questions; from the clients' responses,

---

[28]   Cooperrider, D., & Srivastva, S. (1987). Appreciative Inquiry in organizational life. In Woodman, R., & Pasmore, W. (Eds.), *Research in Organizational Change and Development* (Vol. 1). JAI Press.

the coach and clients chose several themes as the focal points for the rest of the inquiry process.

- **Discover:** Provocative questions are explored regarding each of the Affirmative Topics and, from the clients' responses, the coach and clients again chose several themes. These themes reflect the system's central success factors—its best strengths, talents, assets, values, and ideals—and are known as its positive core.

- **Dream:** Clients use creative processes to verbally and/or experientially explore what the future might be like if the positive core were more thoroughly enacted throughout the system and to examine, looking back from that vantage point, what must have happened to bring it to such an optimal state.

- **Design:** The system is organized into architecture and preferences chosen for each element of that structure that will enable further enactment of the positive core and lessons from the Dream phase throughout the system. Clients may also develop "Provocative Propositions," by putting in writing broad goals or ideas to help encourage the organization to move in the direction of optimization.

- **Destiny:** Concrete plans are made and supporting resources put in place for enacting the chosen preferences in the service of amplifying the positive core and making the clients' dreams a reality. This step involves both the system and the clients.

In the following excerpt from their article "Appreciative Inquiry in Coaching,"[29] Barbara Sloan and Trudy Canine emphasize the significance of the system and highlight the AI principles that are brought to bear on the AI coaching experience:

> AI Coaching is highly effective for a variety of specific coaching purposes, including leadership, transition,

---

[29]   Sloan, B., & Canine, T. (2007, May). Appreciative Inquiry in coaching: Exploration and learnings. *AI Practitioner.* pp. 1–5.

development, working relationships and life planning. The principles of AI influence all stages of AI Coaching, from the initial contact through the final follow-up sessions. The phases of AI guide the general sequence of activities. Both the principles and phases provide guidance in the improvisational dance of the coaching process.

The following describes the impact of the principles of Appreciative Inquiry in AI coaching, adding Wholeness to the well-recognized five principles—Constructionist, Positive, Anticipatory, Simultaneity and Poetic.

- **Constructionist Principle:** The principle of Social Construction recognizes that meaning is made and futures are created through conversations; that our perceptions of reality itself are the product of these conversations; and that our perceived reality defines what we see or do not see (Discover Phase). The stories that are told and retold both formally and informally create and perpetuate the reality of our perceptions. These stories have the power to limit our options as well as to expand the possibilities we can imagine and create. Social construction is happening all the time, everywhere. In organizations, we refer to the socially constructed environment and belief system as the organization's culture. In AI Coaching, we intentionally engage the social system in support of the desired outcomes of the coaching. We use a wide angle lens, if you will, to engage significant others in conversations

- **Positive Principle:** At any moment we can choose to focus on deficits or strengths. From the first contact, including a request for coaching and what might be considered a contracting (Define Phase) conversation, AI Coaching unabashedly focuses on the positive and the strengths, even in the midst of challenges or "problems" that may have led to the request for coaching. Recognizing that each conversation has the capacity to either further cement existing perceptions or to open awareness to strengths and new possibilities, each interaction in AI Coaching is guided by the appreciative principle. Since "we find what we look for," the AI Coach looks for what is appreciative.

- **Anticipatory Principle:** We create what we imagine. As the say goes: "If you're going to have a fantasy, why not go first class?" AI Coaching enables the client to create her/his first class fantasy (Dream Phase), with the support of others whose input and support are important to the client's future. To quote Peter Drucker, great "guru" of the management sciences, "The best way to predict the future is to create it!"

- **Principle of Simultaneity:** Change begins with the first question we ask. So AI Coaching begins by asking questions about the best of times and wishes for the future, even in the face of the habitual inclination in our culture to focus on what's wrong and what's missing—to focus on problems. As Barbara Carpenter, a psychotherapist, says, "It's a new now!" And it is in every moment that we are changing and influencing change. AI Coaching is mindful that moment to moment, in every question we ask or statement we make, we are creating the future for good or ill.

- **Poetic Principle:** With the daily demands for productivity in life and work, the poetic, the artistic, the inspirational can easily be lost. In AI Coaching, we begin by asking for stories rather than for lists or ideas. Thus, the poetic principle seeks to give voice to the poetic impulse, to illuminate aspirations and dreams and to create opportunities for deeper connections between people—all toward the creation of a valued, shared future

- **Principle of Wholeness:** Wholeness acknowledges interconnectedness rather than divisions. Wholeness has a permeable or flexible boundary and is defined and redefined by the focus on inquiry. So in AI Coaching, a client may engage his/her manager and his/her staff in inquiry, later expanding this to include colleagues and clients. By engaging the most appropriate and most whole group of people (rather than a sample) in generative conversations, AI Coaching creates widely shared awareness and appreciation of differing views, shared dreams for the future and greater support for meaningful change.

Now that you have a general understanding of AI, why don't you try the following AI exercise. This will work with any team or group, even if you are not a professional coach. It is also effective if you train coaches.

CBV Reflection ♣ ♠ ♥

Working with AI: A Powerful Example

Ask participants to give you the absolutely worst, most horrible, difficult, hopeless problem they can think of, anywhere in life or work. Often they come up with things like HIV/AIDS, urban violence, corruption, civil war—things like that.

Next do a quick "problem tree" analysis of root causes and their impacts/fruits. Ask the participants about the chances to solve the problem, and at the same time, ask them to draw a face that represents their feelings about these chances. You will normally get a miserable sad face with tears.

Ask the participants to "flip this into an opportunity": "What does the opposite look like?" Defining the problem as its opposite may take a while (in my experience up to an hour). After they've done this, ask the participants to come up with an action plan and personal commitments. This is very often full of energy and fun. Sometimes participants may even choose to create skits and dances. At this moment, do a quick "opportunity tree analysis" and ask for new pictures of faces reflecting how the participants feel about it all. You may get (as expected, of course) lots of smiling, happy faces and great optimism.

Then say, "OK, what happened here? Did the problem go away? Did the world change during the last 60 minutes?" This opens a lively discussion on the heart of AI, how changing our language, our questions, changes reality, and people understand that we have the power to change the world through the questions we ask, through the approach we take. This leads them into taking their organizational "problems," issues, hang-ups, headaches, and hopeless situations and building an AI environment around them.

Exercises like this are often eye-openers. AI is powerful stuff.

Ontological coaching model

Ontological coaching is an eclectic approach. It borrows concepts from PNL, from emotional intelligence, and from the biology of cognition (specifically from the work of holistic living-system scientist, Humberto Maturana).[30] In their book *Understanding Computers and Cognition,* Fernando Flores, a key figure in the development of the ontological approach, and Terry Winograd pulled together the ideas of Maturana with those of philosopher John Searle and came up with the concept of an organization as a "network of commitments." Flores says that in developing the framework for ontological coaching, while he and his colleagues brought together Searle's notions of the philosophy of language and Mantura's ideas about perception, cognition, language, and communication, he was also influenced by the existential philosophy of Martin Heidegger.[31]

Ontology is the study of being, and ontological coaching focuses on all aspects of communication (which are essential aspects of one's "way of being") as a means of producing major shifts in perception and behavior. An individual's way of being can be thought of as the internal reality he or she lives in, which includes—and this is especially important—the relationship the person has with herself. According to Flores and his colleagues,[32] an individual's understanding of the external world and the ways in which he or she participates in it derive from this internal reality.

Ontological coaching is based on the power of language, moods, and conversations to effect behavioral and cultural transformation. The role of an ontological coach is not to tell the client how to be or behave, but rather

---

[30]   Maturana, H. R., & Varela, F. J. (1980). *Autopoiesis and Cognition: The Realisation of the Living.* Dordrecht and Boston: Reidel; Maturana, H. R., & Varela, F. J. (1992). *The Tree of Knowledge: The Biological Roots of Human Understanding* (Rev. ed.). Shambala.

[31]   Heidegger, M. (1962). *Being and Time* (J. Macquarie & E. Robinson, Trans.). Harper.

[32]   Ontological coaching stems from the work of a number of Chileans: Maturana, Flores and Echeverria. Echeverria worked with Flores until he and Julio Olalla decided to go their own way and form The Newfield Group

to help the client to achieve what he or she desires. Ontological coaching is not based on a script the coach has learned in advance. It is about enabling people to better serve themselves, to expand their possibilities, and to increase their capacity to learn, to act more effectively, and to better design their own future. It is more an art than a science.

Way of being, as proponents of ontological coaching define it, is a dynamic interplay between three spheres of human existence: language; moods and emotions; physiology and body posture. A person's way of being shapes his or her performance and effectiveness. Exhibit 1.8 shows us graphically how these three areas are interconnected and that changes made in these areas will result in changes in behavior.

Exhibit 1.8: The three components of the ontology approach to coaching

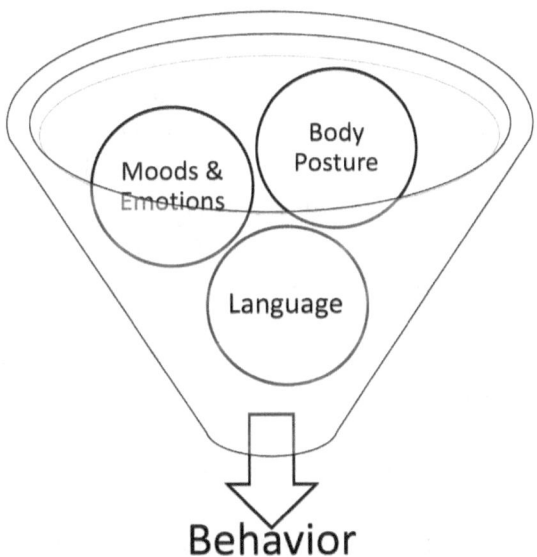

Language

The ontological coaching methodology is based on an understanding of language and communication developed in the latter part of the twentieth century. The essence of this understanding is a) language consists of both listening and speaking and b) language is fundamental in creating reality. Language produces outcomes and generates realities. People act from what reality is for them. Effective behavior depends strongly on people's use of language (including listening). The ways in which people do or do not use language shape what they do and how well they do it.

Included in this methodology is an interpretation of and detailed model of the process of listening. This model provides a deeper and more effective way to listen that enhances communication and relationships. Listening is regarded as a crucial factor in communication and as essential for establishing trust and rapport. Listening is a core business process.

Speaking is also a key business process. This methodology contains six precise linguistic tools (called "basic linguistic acts") that humans use in everyday conversations to create reality and get things done. Typically, people are not aware of how they use and misuse these linguistic tools. Gaining an awareness of how to use them enables people to intentionally produce more effective ways of conversing, relating, and performing in workplace settings.

Stories and narratives are often silent, invisible, and in background of everyday conversations. They reflect the deep culture of organizations and can be major barriers to change. They provide powerful contexts of meaning, shaping what people see as possible and not possible for an individual, a team, or the organization as a whole. The culture—and the shadowy stories that reproduce and reinforce it—can be a limiting horizon or a flexible sense of the possible that encourages improvement throughout the system. A key part of using the ontological methodology is uncovering destructive narratives and developing powerful and empowering narratives.

Moods and emotions

Traditional organizations ignore human emotions. However, the renewed focus on humanity in organizations requires an understanding of human emotions. To energize employees is to harness emotion. Negative emotions have a negative effect on people and on profit; good emotions are fuel that drives productivity, quality, and customer satisfaction. An individual is always in some mood or emotion. Moods and emotions permeate and influence everything people do and as such, they constitute a core business process.

The ontological coaching methodology contains tools for recognizing, managing, and shifting moods and emotions. The power of moods and emotions is that they always predispose people toward certain behaviors and away from others. Speaking, listening, and engaging in conversations, are indispensable forms of human behavior. The effectiveness with which people speak and listen cannot be separated from moods and emotions.

Unfortunately until very recently, moods and emotions were not seen as an area of learning crucial to performance improvement. They are an integral part of using language for effective communication in leadership, management, coaching, and team building. In short, they form a crucial dimension of morale and organizational performance. Tools in this methodology include those that teach people

- how to distinguish between moods and emotions

- how to recognize and use six basic moods of life as a deeper level of emotional intelligence, and how they impact on morale and performance

- how to shift from negative moods to positive moods

- how to use moods and emotions to have more effective and influential communication that builds relationships and long-term collaboration

- how to engage in constructive emotional leadership

Physiology and body posture

This would seem to be an unlikely area of attention in the context of organizational performance and improvement. Like moods and emotions, the body has largely been ignored as a key area affecting individual and organizational performance. The importance of the body can be expressed in the following way: "Our way of being is embodied."

The body is always present in how people listen to each other and speak with each other. Speaking is not limited to the vocal chords; it is generated from the entire body. (Actors and singers know this well.) An individual's posture consists of subtle configurations of muscles and skeleton that have been learned throughout life. In many subtle and powerful ways, posture can keep people trapped in negative moods and negatively impact listening and speaking. Conversely, posture can engender good moods and positively affect listening and speaking.

Specific tools that are part of this aspect of the methodology help people learn

- how to use the body to get into more constructive and productive moods

- how small shifts in body posture can generate a more positive outlook and produce more effective communication

So proponents of ontological coaching assert that organizations and individuals who engage in an ontological coaching relationship can expect to experience different perspectives on personal challenges and opportunities, enhanced thinking and decision-making skills, improved interpersonal effectiveness, and increased confidence in carrying out their chosen work or life roles.

Wellness coaching

Wellness coaching, though not even 20 years old, is a fast-growing industry. Wellness coaches appeal to the current consumer desire for a holistic-and-customized approach to health. They are trained professionals who help clients find ways to pursue healthier lifestyles. They are available to both individuals and to employees—or departments—of an organization.[33]

A wellness coach is not the same as a personal trainer, who primarily develops individualized exercise programs. A wellness coach can work with clients to help them change any of the aspects of their lives that are the most unhealthy, including dietary habits, exercise, and smoking, among others. A good coach won't simply tell a client to drop some behaviors or engage in others. He or she will work with a client to figure

---

[33] For more on wellness coaching, see: Arloski, M. (2007). *Wellness Coaching for Lasting Lifestyle Change*. Whole Person Associates.

out how present life contributes to negative behaviors and to determine what can be done to make behavior change easier. The coach will then create a customized program that addresses diet, fitness, and emotional well-being. Most wellness coaching models that I am aware of require an HRA (health risk assessment), PHA (personal health assessment), or ORA (organizational risk assessment). Each of these not only produces a data set that can be mined to determine program success but also gives the wellness coach a feel for the client's background.

Individual wellness coaching

Despite the significant advances in medical science, many people are still unhealthy. They are overweight, stressed, or indulging in unhealthy behaviors like smoking and excessive alcohol and drug use. Time spent in a doctor's office is usually minimal, and doctors' schedules are so packed that they may address the issue of wellness simply by imploring a patient to live in more intelligent ways or delivering a sound lecture on the evils of certain behaviors. This does not often succeed at producing the desired change. But suggesting a patient get wellness coaching might be.

In the best sense, wellness coaching creates a relationship between coach and client. The coach looks holistically at the person's life prior to helping him or her evolve ideas for changing it. The number of visits and amount of time this could take varies depending on each coach's preferences and the client's individual needs.

Corporate wellness coaching

In organizational wellness, the focus can be on the individual worker (here is where the coach can play a major role) or on units of the organization in which an epidemiological assessment shows high level of risk. The latter is normally handled by HR experts or organizational consultants, who may propose changes in working conditions or other types of remedies. Approaches to wellness vary greatly. Some programs are oriented to "employees at risk" and others are preventive in nature and focus on enhancing well-being.

Wellness coach training

Wellness coaching covers a wide range of activities (personal and organizational), and coaches need to be well trained. As opposed to other coaches, wellness coaches require a background in medicine and psychology as well as in coaching.

Exhibit 1.9 describes the overall content of what is, or should be, addressed during wellness coaching. The goals of the wellness coaching process are the "Desired States" in the graphic. This exhibit is based on a book I am coauthoring with Scott Moodie (in preparation). We are also offering this as a graduate course at ESADE.

Exhibit 1.9: What should be included in wellness coaching?

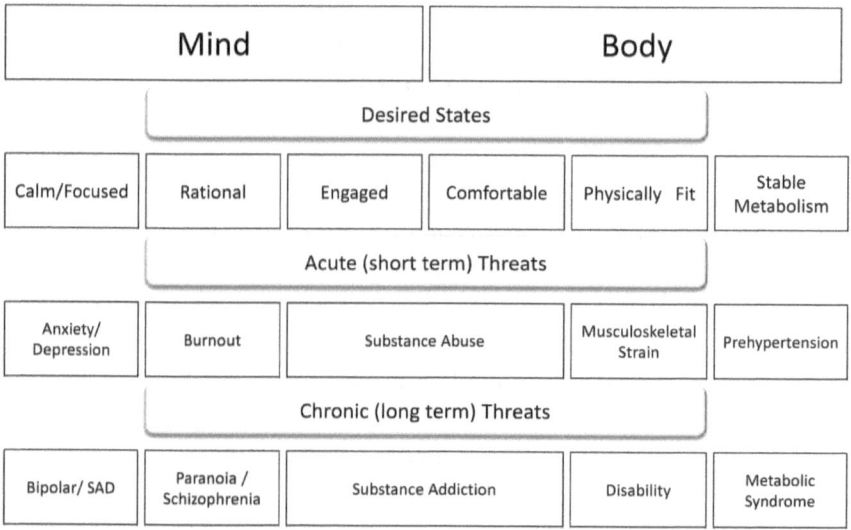

The outline of our proposed ESADE graduate course on wellness coaching will give you an idea of the specific skills a wellness coach needs:

Part 1: Understanding the Foundations of Wellness: The Mind and Body Connections

Part 2: Being a Wellness Coach

Wellness Coaching and Values

Michael Arloski, PhD, PCC, CWP

The field of wellness and health promotion has evolved over the last thirty years to show us that lifestyle is the key determinant for the health of a population and that we need to do much more than simply educate to see behavioral change. The paradigm shift has been towards the individualization of wellness and lasting behavioral change, seeking to reach each person with not just better information, but with working alliances that can help them achieve lasting lifestyle improvement. Those allies accompany the person through the behavioral change process instead of just pointing them in the right direction and encouraging them to succeed alone. We have discovered that the more these allies shift from a medical prescriptive approach, or an educational approach, and instead adopt a coach approach, the more they see actual behavioral change.

Wellness coaching is fast becoming a service offered by corporate wellness programs, disease management companies, employee assistance programs, health insurance companies, and employee wellness programs based in hospitals, educational institutions, and various organizations. Dee Edington, at the University of Michigan's Health Management Research Center, and a pioneer in the field of health risk assessment, has recently made the case for wellness coaching in his new book Zero Trends: Health as a Serious Economic Strategy. He shows us that wellness coaches can help not only those who are at high-risk, but can help "keep the healthy people, healthy" which he states is the best long-range economic and health strategy.

Wellness coaching methodology is very client-centered. Coaches help their clients to 1) take inventory of their health and wellness, then 2) get clear about their own vision of what living a healthy and well life looks like (a well-life vision). Addressing the disparity or gap between where the client is now (current health status) and where they want to be (vision), help the client to form 3) a wellness plan made up of areas they want to focus on to improve their lifestyle. That wellness plan has action steps co-created by both the client and the coach. The coach is then able to 4) help the client be accountable to themselves and gain the support they need to succeed both within the coaching relationship and throughout the rest of their life. Working through both internal and external barriers to change, the coaching ally helps the client to succeed at achieving 5) effective measureable outcomes that improve their lives. As you can see, wellness coaching is not simply a process of goal setting, it is whole-life planning, and at the heart of it are the client's values.

The values and beliefs the client holds about themselves and the world around them drive their attitudes and behavior. The effective wellness coach honors the client's values and helps them examine and clarify their value base. The coach approach maximizes motivation by having the client set the agenda for change and co-create the wellness plan with the coach, rather than pushing a pre-packaged "how-to-be-well" program for the client to follow. The client's values are foundational to all of the choices and all the prioritization that takes place.

Wellness coaches begin by honoring what is. They honor the client values and do not attempt to replace them with their own. A real valuable process the coach offers, however is to help the client to 1) clarify what their values really are and to 2) examine how self-enhancing (and health-enhancing) or self-defeating their values are. They also can 3) help their clients gain insight into ways that they are living which are incongruent with their values and hence are a source of tremendous stress and conflict. For example, a client may have grown up valuing self-sufficiency to such a degree that they are unwilling to ask for, or receive the help they need. Without social support their efforts at changing behavior perpetually fail. The coach does not identify this self-defeating behavior and label it as such, but instead asks the client to examine how holding such a strong value works for them in some ways, but may be working against them when it comes to improving their quality of life and their health.

Exploring and examining such lifestyle-related values can be challenging for both the coach and client. Our ways of living are often based on values learned and adopted from our familial, cultural, and religious backgrounds. These values are then expressed in the norms of our peers. Peer health norms are widely known to be powerful influences on our health choices. It can be very difficult to be the only family member working at improving her diet. Being surrounded by friends whose style of recreation is always sedentary can make adopting physically active pursuits challenging. At the same time, it is often peers who can provide the support clients need to achieve success at lifestyle improvement. If a client's family members or coworkers encourage and praise health-enhancing behaviors—such as being more physically active, eating in a healthy way, not smoking, and the like—the client will find it much easier to adopt those behaviors. Wellness coaches can help their clients expand their peer groups, learn to ask for the help they need, and develop strategies for dealing with negative peer health norms.

Wellness coaching clients often find that the process of self-assessment/self-exploration, clarifying a well-life vision, and co-creating a behaviorally based wellness plan is in fact a gigantic values clarification exercise! When coaches ask, "What do you really want?" the client has to connect with values at a core level. When coaches help people remember how truly free they are to make their own choices, they examine automatic default behaviors and either embrace or reject them. Throughout this process of change, the client enjoys the support of a real ally who expresses genuine caring and compassion.

The values that the wellness coach expresses are found not in clinical or health professional recommendations or prescriptions, nor are they found in mere coaching techniques. They are found in the ways of being that make them effective coaches. Effective coaches value the same things that psychologist Carl Rogers found long ago were the keys to effective therapy, what he called "the facilitative conditions of therapy" and we can just as easily call "the facilitative conditions of coaching." Empathy, warmth, unconditional positive regard, and being genuine enhance the coaching relationship and allow the client to grow. Providing these conditions is not done by practicing techniques but rather by holding such values and living them. The best coaches develop the ability not only to hold such values but to express them in the coaching sessions with their clients. When clients experience deeper levels of acceptance, honesty, trust, compassion, and A web of values is interlaced throughout the wellness coaching process. The values of the client, the values in the client's environment, and the values of the coach affect the process of working toward lifestyle improvement. By including values in the coaching process in a very conscious way, we can enhance the probability of successfully achieving lasting lifestyle change.

Michael Arloski, PhD, PCC, CWP, is a licensed psychologist, professional certified coach, and certified wellness practitioner. He is CEO of Real Balance Global Wellness Services, in Colorado (www.realbalance.com). Over 2,000 wellness coaches have been trained by his company worldwide. Dr. Arloski is the author of numerous wellness publications, including *Wellness Coaching for Lasting Lifestyle Change* (Duluth MN: Whole Person Associates), the leading book in the wellness coaching field.

1.5 On coaches, professionalism, and professional associations

Today, anyone can call himself or herself a coach. There are no rules, regulations, laws, restrictions, or enforced codes. Personal coaching produced a startling number of successes in its early years. Since then many people have jumped on the bandwagon to take advantage of the good name that these successes created. Now, these people, all calling themselves coaches, offer a myriad of different coaching methods, styles, philosophies, structures, ethics, backgrounds, niches, and purposes.

The coaching community itself is confused about what constitutes coaching and how to determine what the coaching process is. Vicki Brock pointed this out in her 2008 doctoral dissertation on the history of coaching,[34] "Inside the field there is much divergent thinking of what

---

[34]   Brock, V. (2008). *Grounded theory of the roots and emergence of coaching* (Unpublished doctoral dissertation), pp. 2, 6. International University of Professional Studies, Hawaii.

coaching is and whose approach is best. Outside the field there is even more confusion among clients and the public about what makes up coaching." This is compounded by the existence of "many definitions of coaching, some of which contradict each other, are based on and influenced by practitioners' backgrounds, theories, and models."

Government bodies have not found it necessary to provide a regulatory standard for coaching, nor does any state body govern the education or training standard for the coaching industry; the title "coach" can be used by any service provider. Critics charge that life coaching is akin to psychotherapy without restrictions, oversight, or regulation. The state legislature of Colorado, after holding a hearing on such concerns, disagreed asserting that coaching is unlike therapy because it does not focus on examining or diagnosing the past. Instead coaching focuses on effecting change in a client's current and future behavior. Additionally, life coaching does not include diagnosing mental illness or dysfunction.

Sociologists many years ago developed criteria for assessing professionals. Some of these are a common body of knowledge, a minimum requirement (and testing or certification) to enter the profession and a clear code of ethics. Those who criticize "coaching" as a profession claim that as of today coaches do not meet any of these criteria (as distinguished from medical doctors or psychologists, for example).

The International Coaching Federation (ICF) has created a code of ethics—and does certify coaches—but does not have the capacity to enforce its code or follow up on its certification (by, for instance, requiring recertification after a period of time or insisting continuing education be a basis for keeping one's certification). Only a small segment of the coaches worldwide even bother to become members of the ICF. Moreover, the public at large isn't aware of its existence. Likewise, the International Coaching Community (ICC), which claims to be the largest such organization in the world (6,000 coaches in 60 countries), has developed a code of standards and ethics but admittedly cannot enforce it. The ICC's code comprises four sections: Professional Conduct at Large, Conflicts of Interest, Professional Conduct with Clients and Confidentiality/Privacy. I hope—and it's safe to say that many, if not most, professional coaches share my hope—that in the future governments will step in and create some order in the field.

1.6 Selecting your coaching model

How do you select *your model* of coaching (whether you are a professional coach or not) when so many models are available?

We have seen that the coaching discipline integrates several fields of knowledge, each having its own schools of thought, models, and theories. This may seem confusing, even daunting, but it opens a world of opportunities. If you learn about different models—mining their unique elements while noticing what they have in common—you can incorporate aspects of them into your coaching approach to craft a flexible methodology that will work for you.

Creating an *entire* model from scratch is extremely difficult, but being locked into one model can severely limit you. The fluid, shifting, and various nature of the circumstances you will encounter while coaching will frequently leave you stumped if you are wedded to a single model, a single way of doing things. But it is important that you remain mindful of the essential elements that effective coaching approaches share. To be successful, a coaching process must be based on these three pillars:

- the establishment of a relationship built on trust, genuine communication, and confidentiality

- the formulation of client-based, agreed-upon goals and expectations

- a deep questioning and learning dynamic in relation to clients' goals

In addition, a coaching process needs to have models and methods that address the following areas:[35]

> **Advanced communication model—for a focused conversation:** Coaching is a *highly focused conversation, a* specialized communication that gets to the heart of things

---

[35] Adapted from: Meta-Coach Foundation (MCF). Coaching Models. http://www.meta-coachfoundation.org/index.php?option=com_content&task=view&id=34&Itemid=57.

as a client explores dreams, hopes and values. An advanced model for communication is essential to quickly and incisively getting to the core issues. Otherwise, the coaching degenerates into "a nice chat."

Reflexivity model—for facilitating emotional intelligence: Coaching involves and facilitates a client's *stepping back to the thoughts in the back of the mind.* Bringing out the reflexive thinking of the self-dialogue that goes on simultaneously in the back of one's mind is an important element in getting to the crux of things in the coaching process.

The kind of consciousness that humans have is very special. It self-reflexive consciousness. This speaks about the human ability to think-about-our-thinking, to feel-about-our-feelings, and to respond to our responses. A professional coach will have studied the principles of meta-cognition and use a meta-cognitive reflexivity model for efficiently and effectively facilitating this degree of awareness.

Generative change model—for facilitating change: Coaching first and foremost deals with performance change (a change in one's quality and level of performance), but it does not stop there. A coach also works with developmental change—for example, the changes necessary when a client needs to evolve his or her sense of identity, beliefs, and values. Nor does it stop there. An even higher level of change is transformational change. This speaks about changing one's direction, purpose, mission, and vision. These multidimensional levels of change indicate the generative change of coaching and call for a model of generative change so that a coach can determine the level of change a client is seeking and how to facilitate it.

Most coaching change models come from therapy change models rather than change models specifically designed for the healthy self-actualizing person, a person who embraces change rather than fights it. In fact, this is one of the two key differences between generative change and the remedial change of therapy. In therapeutic models of change, clients are expected to resist and relapse. Not so in a generative model of change. If a coach is a change agent, he or she will obviously have to know how to dance with the mechanisms of change for a healthy person who simply wants to unleash more of his or her potential, and will work from a coaching change model that specifically deals with this kind of change.

Implementation model—for measuring change: Coaching, while a conversation, is not merely about talking; the bottom line of coaching is *doing*. An effective coach is able to bring about change by enabling and empowering a client to actually incorporate the change and embody it in his or her physiology. In this way the coach facilitates implementation of the great ideas, visions, and values talked about in the coaching session. Coaching is ultimately about actualizing potentials and visions. It is about executing the co-created action plans and following through to ensure the client makes them real (i.e., realizes them in his or her life). An effective coach needs several models for implementing ideas and visions. At the most fundamental level, there needs to be a personal implementation that empowers the client to *embody* the changes so that they become part of his or her way of being in the world. Next, there needs to be a way to mark and measure the change, a way to benchmark even intangible and conceptual principles so that one can know that all the talk during the coaching sessions actually makes a difference. This requires an explicit implementation model for measuring change.

Systems model—for systemic change: The process has to be systemic in nature because coaching works with the whole person, the mind-body-and-emotion within many systems—relational, family, work, cultural, and organizational, among others. A coach has to be able to think, speak, and work systemically with clients. To that end, an effective coach needs a systemic model that enables him or her to see and work with multiple systems simultaneously. This is critical for ecological reasons and it is crucial to effectiveness.

To work systemically is to energize the person's mind-body-and-emotion system so that what is imagined and envisioned becomes a congruent change fully aligned within all the contexts and relationships of life.

Self-actualization model—for unleashing potential: Coaching depends on a unique form of psychology. Not abnormal psychology, which deals with neurosis and psychosis; not even normal psychology, which deals with the average. It deals with the healthy person who is self-actualizing to become his or her best. It deals with the psychology of the person seeking excellence. The kind of human psychology an effective coach uses works to unleash potentials so that a client will activate his or her best and experience peak performance.

This kind of psychology is self-actualization psychology as pioneered by Abraham Maslow (we will discuss his hierarchy of needs theory in the next chapter) others, part of the Human Relations Movement. Given this psychology informs most coaching, the professional coach will work from the current self-actualizing models in the field.

Conclusion

In this chapter, I offered an overview of the coaching discipline—presenting several coaching types, approaches, and models. This review wasn't meant to be exhaustive, but rather to be a jumping off point for your own research. Looking at these coaching approaches and briefly at the standards and guidelines created by international coaching federations gave us a basic understanding of the competencies that all effective coaches must have and the features that successful coaching processes share.

But there is a key point that I haven't yet addressed—a question each individual needs to ask before choosing an approach, Do I want to apply the model to myself or to others whom I would like to help?

As I said earlier, with few exceptions all people can be coaches, at least to themselves and to their immediate families, friends, and colleagues at work. But some methods and tools require more training than others. While I have been trained in hypnotherapy, I use the technique only for self-hypnosis or with my family, my relatives, and my children. I don't think I am qualified to use hypnotherapy as a professional. Coaching models vary in terms of their assumptions, complexities, and readiness for use. Not all can be picked up and followed step-by-step or simply imposed as is on a situation. Here are some thoughts about coaching models that I find helpful:

- They serve only as tools for coaches

- They are limited by cultural factors that influence coaching beliefs and practices (both for the coaches and for the coachees)

- There is no one particular model that is the best nor is there one right way to coach

- Remember: Coaches learn and coaching models evolve

- Start from where you are and where you feel comfortable

What lies ahead in coaching? I think one of the best ways of looking at the future is to quote one of the founders of this profession, John Whitmore. Whitmore says:[36]

> The coaching profession faces many challenges and huge opportunities, and a great responsibility. It has grown from personal coaching to group coaching. From a cottage industry

---

[36]   Whitmore, J. (2009). Will coaching rise to the challenge? *The OCM Coach and Mentor Journal*, 92–93.

to a workplace profession; can it now shed the inevitable self-limiting beliefs of an expanding role to become a global force to serve humanity on a big scale and on the front line? What coaching has to offer is the means to construct exactly what is most needed all over this time, the individual and collective responsibility essential for the survival of life as we know it.

Another approach to coaching: In the remainder of the book, I will present another approach to coaching, one that is based on values. My experience has shown that focusing on values offers a parsimonious, simple, and easy-to-follow framework that produces deep, lasting, and generative change.

The Coaching by Values model is based on three fundamental principles: 1) a presentation of distinct concept that explains why values should be the cornerstone of a coaching effort, specifically when the coach attempts to bring about positive changes in the coachee's life (be it at work or in other settings); 2) a clear description of the process and methodology for applying the CBV model; and 3) concrete practical tools that enable the coach to get results efficiently and effectively.

If you are open to these ideas and think you'll benefit from CBV, please read on. I will present it in detail, so don't worry if this is unfamiliar territory. But remember the importance of the sequence. Please do not jump ahead before you really understand the foundations. After explaining the logic, I will provide you with a step-by-step methodology for applying it. I will not deceive you and leave you with only the theory. My proposed method also involves performing steps within a specific sequence, but within that sequence there is room for great creativity. So, let's begin the "voyage."

In the next chapter, I will show just how powerful words are as we explore the concepts "values" and "value." In chapter 3, I'll introduce you to the 3Es tri-axial model that is the basis of the CBV methodology. In chapter 4, I will go step-by-step through the CBV method, applying it to both personal and work situations. In chapter 5, I will take the risk of looking at the future—of values, of CBV, and of the world. But now, let us begin the Coaching by Values journey.

CBV Reflection ♣ ♠ ♥

Think of the key message(s) you retained after reading this chapter. Then complete the following sentences:

The principal points I liked in this chapter include

1._____
2._____
3._____

The principal points that I did not like or disagreed with in this chapter include

1._____
2._____
3._____

This part to be completed only if you are already a professional coach:

After reading this chapter, I am more convinced that (select only one and explain)

    a.   The coaching method(s)/philosophy I use really works and I do not need to broaden it because

       _____
       _____
       _____

    b.   The coaching method(s)/philosophy I use works relatively well, but I am willing to incorporate complementary approaches because

       _____
       _____
       _____

    c.   Wow!!! I realize how incomplete my method(s)/philosophy is. I am willing to search for better or complementary methods, because

       _____
       _____
       _____

Chapter 2
Coaching and Values,
or the Value of Values[37]

- 2.1 Natural system and human system:
  The DNA called "values"

- 2.2 The ABC of values

- 2.3 Value formation

- 2.4 Modeling the universe of values: The 3Es tri-axial
  approach

- 2.5 Values and culture

- Conclusion

---

[37] The "Value of Values" is a registered trademark of Gestion MDS Inc. of
Montreal and Simon L. Dolan in Canada and Spain (© 2010). Used with
permission.

2.1 Natural system and human system: The DNA called "values"

The natural system—the universe, the solar system, the earth—is composed of time, space and material; it is the most basic world of existence, and it provides living organisms with the fundamentals they need for their existence. If there were no land, water, air or light, the universe would become an empty space in which no life could exist.[38]

The natural system generates living organisms, letting them grow or become extinct, by physically sustaining its constant state or changing itself, or chemically combining or dissolving its various elements. The stars are moving, exploding or transforming themselves in the apparently boundless universe by immeasurable mysterious power. The stars have limitless power and values over the humans as well as all the other living organisms on the earth. These stars have values of sustenance and change, values of combination and dissolution, values of conservation and generation, and values of standstill and movement. Weight, energy, objects and light realize various values.

Tong-Keun Min formerly of Chung Nam University, Korea (see second footnote in this chapter), has classified values by such qualities as individual and social, natural and artificial, and personal and impersonal. The following is a partial list of the classes of values he's identified:

- individual values and social values

- natural values and artificial values

- physical values and mental values

---

[38] NOTE: This section was greatly inspired by the writings of Tong-Keun Min of Chung Nam National University, Korea, in particular *A Study on the Hierarchy of Values* (http://www.bu.edu/wcp/Papers/Valu/ValuMin.htm), the excellent presentation he gave at the Twentieth World Congress of Philosophy (1998, Aug. 10–15, Boston). I made numerous attempts to contact the author and obtain permission to begin this chapter with his beautiful description of values and the natural system, but was unable to reach him. A Korean doctoral student at ESADE has been graciously assisting me in this effort and discovered that Tong-Keun retired from the university in 1995. I will continue to try to reach him to obtain his explicit permission for future editions.

- instrumental values and intrinsic values

- temporary values and permanent values

- exclusive values and universal values

- lower values and higher values

- unproductive values and productive values

- active values and inactive values

- personal values and impersonal values

- theoretical values and practical values

- relative values and absolute values

Values are indeed manifold and countless, and values in an individual's life are interconnected. For example, artistic values and social values depend on physical values, because we can not engage in artistic or social activities without our lives or bodies. Science, education, and political activities depend, more or less, on economic values, because we need some degree of economic support for these. Intellectual values and political values influence our economy just as a remarkable talent or an excellent policy can make a home or a nation prosperous.

Values are strategic lessons learned and maintained. They remain relatively stable over time. These lessons teach us that one way of acting is better than its opposite if we are to achieve our desired outcome(s)—that is, our values and value systems guide our behavior toward that which we think will turn out well for us. Thus, to the extent that they constitute deliberate or preferentially strategic choices, in the medium to long term, for certain ways of behaving and against others, toward the survival or *good life* of a particular system, values form the nucleus, the DNA, of human liberty.

Today the human race faces a multitude of potentially catastrophic problems: environmental pollution, human alienation and unemployment, the depletion of natural resources, crimes, drug addiction, megacities, exploding populations, the disintegration of the family, mistreatment of the elderly, the threat of weapons of mass destruction, unequal distribution of wealth, food, educational opportunities, and resources, and many more.

These challenges cause chaos and disturb established senses of values across cultures. In this chaos, we are losing our reference point.[39]

Solving these problems will require both individual and group efforts, the efforts and cooperation of social organizations, government agencies, business leaders, the academic community and international organizations. At the core of these efforts must be healthy, sustainable values. Educating and enlightening citizens so that they are guided by conscience rather than compulsion will be an important step in activating these values.

2.2 The ABC of values[40]

In many of my previous writings I've stressed the importance of understanding personal values, getting clear about what is most important to us in our life in general (including family and friends) and in our work. But in over 30 years of research on values, I have not yet come across a credible source that tackles this critical concept with sufficient depth. Most of the value research coverage takes you through a process of eliciting your current values and leaves it at that.

In the past 10 years, I've developed a concept, methodology, and tools for engaging in culture reengineering, primarily in corporations. Extensive global experience (several continents, many countries, and multiple cultures) has led me to the conclusion that changing a company's culture always starts with a micro-change in a corporate leader's values. Only when a leader starts to understand his or her own values, modify or adjust them if necessary, and connect them in a holistic way with the organization and/or its stakeholders can the candid journey to change and value alignment really begin. Until then, all attempts at culture change remain superficial; even in the best possible scenario, any attempt at culture change—if not ignited by a shift in the leader's values—will stall far short of the height of excellence it was designed to achieve.

---

[39] For more on these issues, read: Raich, M. & Dolan, S. L. (2008). *Beyond: Business and Society in Transformation*. London: Palgrave Macmillan.

[40] This section has been greatly inspired by my previous writings, specifically Dolan, S. L., Garcia, S., & Richley, B. (2006). *Managing by Values* (chapter 2). London: Palgrave Macmillan; Dolan, S. L., & Lingham, T. (2008). *Fundamentals of International Organizational Behavior* (chapter 10). Sara Books.

Leaders in today's world often ask themselves, "Who am I?" and "What am I to do?" In past decades, leadership depended on institutional and bureaucratic power, but now leadership depends on the capacity to articulate and inspire an organization's mutually selected values.[41] Values, once considered "too soft" to be considered in any serious approach to management, have become a central part of organizational strategy. But there is still long way to go.

In this chapter, I will extrapolate from my experiences with leaders in organizations and delve much deeper into this rich subject. I will examine the concepts of "values" and "value," looking at their genesis and the relationship between values, beliefs, attitudes, and norms. I will then introduce you to the tri-axial model, a framework for intelligently identifying our values and understanding their significance in our lives. This model will give us a means to detect and classify not only our personal values but also those of systems, such as the family, our work environment, society, and so on. We can also use it to determine whether our values are likely to lead us to our goals and whether our current goals are in fact those that will truly fulfill us.

Achieving relative happiness and fulfillment requires aligning our values with our goals and then seeing how the systems in which we live and work are congruent (or not) with these. In the following chapters, I will discuss this in depth. I will also offer methodologies and tools to achieve value alignment—using the tri-axial model as a fundamental steppingstone in the process of Coaching by Values, or CBV.

Values: But what are they?

If you go into any bookstore that specializes in management and inquire about books on values, chances are you will be sent first to the section on stock markets or to the section on business ethics and ethical investment. You will find books about share values (the worth of a share in a corporation) and books dealing with the relationship between values and

---

[41]   See, for example: Dolan, S. L., & Richley, B. (2006). Management by Values (MBV): A new philosophy for a new economic order. *Handbook of Business Strategy*, *7*(1), 235–238; Raich, M., & Dolan, S. L. (2009). Managing in the new landscape. *Effective Executive*, *12*(10), 48–56; Ulrich, D., & Ulrich, W. (2010). *The Why of Work*. McGraw-Hill.

business results. In these books, you will come across several interpretations of the word *value*.

Values are not only words. Values guide and direct our behavior and affect our daily experiences. But the words we use to identify our values and the definitions that we assign to them are particularly powerful; they give meaning to and direct the channeling of human efforts, both on the personal and organizational levels.

The term *axiology* refers to the study of values, and originates from the Greek *axios*, "valuable, estimable or worthy of being honored." Significantly, it is also the root of the English word *axis*, the point around which the essential elements turn.

Milton Rockeach of the University of Minnesota is a world authority on the study of values. His definitions[42] of "value" and "value system" have become classics:

> A value is an enduring belief that a specific mode of conduct or end-state of existence is personally or socially preferable to an opposite or converse mode of conduct or end-state of existence. A value system is an enduring organization of beliefs concerning preferable modes of conduct or end-states of existence along a continuum of relative importance. (*The Nature of Human Values*, p. 5)

In many Latin languages, the words *value* and *valor* (from the Latin *valēre*, "to be worthy; to be strong") represent three different but complementary meanings that can be categorized in the following dimensions:

- **Axiological dimension:** In Greek, *axios* means "worthy" or "worthy of dignity"; it also signifies a focal point or center around which other elements turn.

- **Economic dimension:** In this sense, value is a criterion used to evaluate things in terms of costs, benefits and relative worth, as in today's expression, the "added value" of a person to a firm.

---

[42]   Rockeach, M. (1973). *The Nature of Human Values*. Free Press.

- **Psychological dimension:** Equated with ethics, this dimension also includes the courage that moves companies and people forward in confronting new frontiers without fear.

Similarly, one can look at the definition of values through three perspectives that, as we will see later, are the foundation of the tri-axial model of values: the economic-pragmatic, the ethical-social, and the emotional-developmental.

The economic-pragmatic dimension: Worth

From an economic perspective, "value" is the measure of the significance or importance of something. In this sense, values are criteria used to evaluate things with respect to their relative merit, adequacy, scarcity, price, or interest. By "things" here, I mean people, objects, ideas, actions, feelings, and facts. For example, one may speak of the value of mutual confidence, of the value of creativity at work, or of the value a particular process adds to the products the customer buys. One can also talk of the value of money, the value of a machine, or the value of a particular expert working for the firm.

"Value analysis" refers to the process by which one determines if a product or service is generating optimal customer or user satisfaction at the minimum cost. It is important to note that it is human values like creativity, confidence in the company, and commitment that activate and sustain the behaviors and actions that add value to a product. In fact, "continuous improvement," which became so popular in the management jargon of the 1990s, is based on a set of values.

Another economic concept is the "chain of value," which is the linked set of a company's activities, logistics, operations, and marketing that add or subtract value to a product, leading to the total or final value of the product. According to Michael Porter from Harvard, the chain of value of a company is a reflection of its history and strategy and is a critical and differentiating element for achieving competitive advantage.[43]

But even more important, the chain of value of a company is a reflection of the shared values of the people that constitute the company.

---

[43] Porter, M. L. (1985). *Competitive Advantage: Creating and Sustaining Superior Performance.* Free Press.

Lack of shared values damages a company's value chain, like in the old (but appropriate) adage, "A chain is only as strong as its weakest link." Ask yourself: What are the weak links in my company value chain? How does this impact the *value* of my organization? This same logic can apply to your personal or family life: What constitutes the weak links in your relationships or your family value chain? How does this impact the *value* of your relationships or your family?"

The ethical-social dimension: Preferential choices

Under this concept, an individual might choose quality in work or life in preference to its opposite, the botched, improvised, or rushed job. Similarly, genuine concern for people in the company or family might be preferable to feelings of contempt or indifference. Other examples of these values are the creation of wealth rather than ruin or destruction; autonomy (healthy independence) instead of unhealthy dependence; honesty as opposed to fraudulence; team spirit and cooperation versus individualism. Our true, or core, values are revealed through our actions rather than our words, or what we merely state as being a value.

Values that are demonstrated through behavior are "lived values." "Espoused values" are those that are expressed, either verbally or in writing, but are not consistently embodied or realized in action. An example of a person expressing espoused values is the individual who adamantly states that health is his or her number one value but goes on to smoke cigarettes, take harmful drugs, or never exercise. Similarly, an organization might have a company values statement that lists honesty as its highest value while it engages in questionable bookkeeping practices or withholds critical information from employees or other stakeholders. In both cases, the values are espoused values: They look good on paper or sound good in conversation, but they fail the test of consistent and enduring lived behavior. In essence, espoused values represent a mismatch between what we say and what we do.

Respected sociologist Floyd Henry Allport said that when there are no clearly formulated value options in a society, the society is said to be "anomic."[44] Organizational anomia exists when an organization has no

---

[44]   Allport, F. H. (1924). *Social Psychology.* Houghton Mifflin.

articulated and shared values, when values do not *mean* (in both senses of the word—semantically and in terms of their worth) the same thing throughout the organization. Anomia helps explain the lack of vitality, collective coherence, morale, and unwillingness to make an effort that can be observed in many companies today. Understanding the various types and definitions of values can help individuals and organizations develop a common language about an often fuzzy, complex, and critical aspect of personal and professional lives. Thus values can either be a strong link between people and their organization or the weak link that breaks this all-important bond.

The emotional-developmental dimension: Personal fulfillment

The notion of what constitutes individual happiness and fulfillment varies from person to person, from culture to culture. The emotional-developmental values are those related to freedom and happiness, or more broadly, to personal fulfillment. They represent the type of passion that motivates and sustains people who are trying to realize a dream. Walt Disney believed "all our dreams can come true if we have the courage to pursue them." And Martin Luther King famously declared, "I have a dream that one day on the red hills of Georgia the sons of former slaves and the sons of former slave owners will be able to sit down together at the table of brotherhood."

When one is confident about his or her emotional-developmental values, dreams that once seemed too risky or too far beyond one's capabilities now appear not only reasonable but compelling. This security allows one to live up to one's potential and accomplish dreams that in earlier stages of one's life may have been too frightening to embrace.

Passion and creativity are becoming the most characteristic descriptors for the increasingly educated segment of Western society, say sociologist Paul H. Ray and psychologist Sherry Ruth Anderson, who coined the term "Culture Creatives" to describe the 50 million adult Americans—and an estimated 80 to 90 million Europeans—who since the 1960s have moved beyond the dueling paradigms "progressive" and "conservative."[45] Values

---

[45]   Ray, P. H., & Anderson, S. R. (2000). *The Cultural Creatives: How 50 Million People Are Changing the World.* Harmony Books.

connected with personal fulfillment might be some of the best indicators of behavior, they say, adding that Cultural Creatives attach great significance to the following:

- authenticity (actions must be consistent with words and beliefs)

- engaged action and whole process learning (seeing the world as interwoven and connected)

- idealism and activism (including helping others and valuing their unique gifts)

- concern that business and society overemphasize making money and consuming

- support for the common good

- global issues and ecology

- elevating the importance of women

Not everyone, however, agrees that education and values connected to personal fulfillment are markers of concern for the environment, compassion for the disenfranchised, and disregard for the act of consuming as an end in itself. At the same time that Ray and Anderson have found more and more people who are actively supporting such values and beliefs, the disparity between the classes in the United States has become a yawning chasm. Economists like Nobel laureate Joseph Stiglitz argue that this growing inequality is stifling innovation and constricting opportunities, as the wealthy (and those who emulate them) lose empathy for others, lack interest in the common good, and value profits over planet and people.[46]

---

[46] Stiglitz, J. E. (2011, May). Of the 1%, by the 1%, for the 1%. *Vanity Fair*, pp.126–129.
http://www.vanityfair.com/society/features/2011/05/top-one-percent–201105.

Values, beliefs, norms, attitudes, and behavior

There are three important concepts taken from the general literature in psychology that are closely related to values; these must be understood both as concepts and in their relation to each other—that is, the sequence in which they are formed (see exhibit 2.1)—to implement the Coaching by Values method. These are beliefs, norms, and attitudes.

What are beliefs?

I have said that values may be generally understood as the strategic choices we make regarding what is required to achieve our goals. It is important to recognize that these choices, in turn, are derived from basic suppositions or beliefs about human nature and the world around us. In short, each person chooses to think and act in specific ways according to what he or she believes about people, things, events, ideas, and the world.

One very common assumption is that beliefs are the same as supposed "truths." However, beliefs are deeply rooted structures of thought that we develop over years of learning and experience to explain and make sense of our reality. These structures precede the formulation of our values. For example, being convinced that never having enough time is a sign that someone is successful may encourage one to hold the value that hard work is worthwhile. Believing that what counts are immediate results could support one's valuing immediate benefits, speed in production or work, and even, perhaps, a quick botch job over a quality outcome that takes longer to achieve. Believing that poor quality results in a higher cost in the long run will likely lead to one's embracing good quality as a value.

The relationship between beliefs and values is extremely close. For this reason, in this chapter, I speak of "changes in beliefs and values" much more often than changes in values alone. And throughout the process of Coaching by Values, it is important to keep in mind that beliefs precede values, so a shift in values requires a shift in beliefs. As illustrated in exhibit 2.1, the unlearning of some beliefs is essential if one is to replace or renew values, change behaviors, and be a positive influence.

Exhibit 2.1: Sequence from beliefs to outcomes

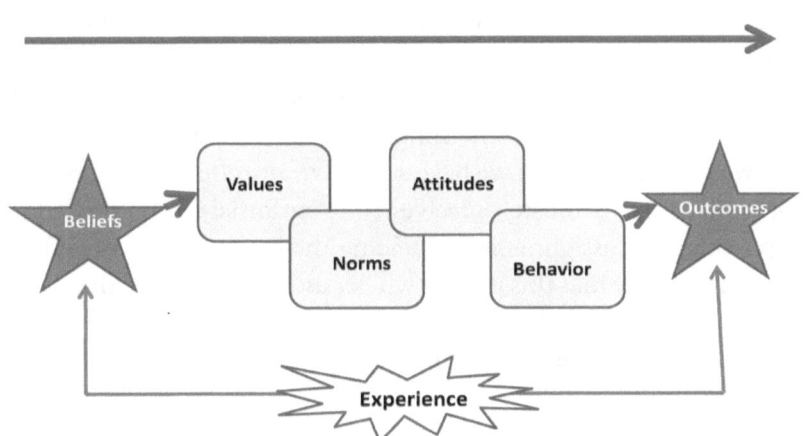

Norms and values

Values play a special role in the formation of norms, or the so-called rules of the game. Our values inform us about what we believe is ethical, good, valid, competitive, appropriate, beautiful, and desirable; they are continually being generated and reinforced throughout our lives. Values are held at the level of the individual; norms tend to emerge from group interactions. Norms are rules of conduct adopted by consensus, whereas values are criteria for evaluating, accepting, or rejecting norms. Further, noncompliance with norms usually incurs external sanctions (e.g., ostracism, fines, imprisonment), whereas noncompliance with values results in feelings of guilt or "internal" sanctions.

Attitudes and values

Often the concept "change of attitude" is used wrongly to refer to the change of something else, namely a change in values, conduct, beliefs, or behaviors. Consider these examples: a change of values such as commitment; a change of conduct such as lack of punctuality; a change of beliefs such as "it is dangerous to detect errors in others and then publicize them." This is partly the result of the popularization of the concept "attitudes" and of trendy uses of "change in attitude" (for example, in social surveys). Usually the confusion originates from researchers in the field of management or psychology who find it easier to measure attitudes than values.

An attitude is a consequence of the values and norms that precede it. It is an evaluating factor or tendency, either positive or negative, toward other people, deeds, events, things, and so on. Our attitudes reflect how we feel toward someone or something and predict our tendency to act in a certain way. For example, if we have a positive attitude toward a particular job or project and dedicate ourselves to it enthusiastically; this conduct (e.g., pursuing the assignment, embracing the hard work involved) stems from the possibility that this project will let us to put into practice a certain value (e.g., creativity), which in turn stems from certain beliefs (e.g., we must be creative in order to thrive in our market, creativity is personally fulfilling).

Attitudes and behavior

Attitude is a feeling, or opinion, of approval or disapproval toward something. Behavior is an action or reaction that occurs in response to an event or internal stimuli (e.g., thought). People hold complex relationships between attitudes and behavior that are further complicated by the social factors influencing both. Behaviors usually, but not always, reflect established beliefs, values, and attitudes. But behavior can be influenced by a number of factors beyond attitude: preconceptions about self and others, monetary factors, social influences or norms (what peers and community members are saying and doing), and convenience, among others. For example, in a society in which premarital abstinence is embedded as a value, a man who believes strongly in abstinence before marriage may choose to remain a virgin until his wedding night. But if that society is rife with messages tying masculinity to sexual activity, that same man may engage in premarital sex, succumbing to these social messages despite both his convictions and the avowed values of his society.

Ideally, positive attitudes manifest well-adjusted behaviors. But in some cases, healthy attitudes may result in harmful behavior. For example, someone may remain in an abusive and potentially deadly domestic situation because he or she holds negative attitudes toward divorce.

Studies have clearly demonstrated that in some cases pointing out inconsistencies between attitudes and behavior can redirect the behavior.

And some coaches focus on changing attitudes in order to change behavior. This is the essence of cognitive-behavior therapy, which combines two types of techniques: those designed to change irrational ways of thinking (e.g., attitudes and/or beliefs)[47] and those aimed directly at correcting the resulting inappropriate behavior.[48] Actually, this approach works well in many cases, but I've found that rather than attempting to change attitudes to modify behavior, it is more effective to modify the values and beliefs that underlie the conduct. This produces deep, lasting change. The process, however, is more complex.

The stress connection

In an ideal world, everyone would be able to create environments in which his or her beliefs, values, norms, attitudes, and behaviors were perfectly aligned. But rarely is reality so neat. Demands on our lives and work are increasing more rapidly than ever. Factors such as globalization, new technologies, heightened competitiveness, mounting pressure on companies to do more with less, the growing premium on multitasking, and organizations that increasingly require each individual to accomplish tasks once divided among several people have created a world in which people are perpetually "on call." Rarely are any of us unplugged from the perpetual motion swirling around us. The convergence of these dynamics activates—and by activating, brings into strong relief—a basic relationship between beliefs, values, and behavior: stress.

Today stress is usually referred to as "the entire process by which people perceive and interpret their environment in relation to their capability to cope with it."[49] Under this definition, stress is present when the environment poses (or is perceived to pose) a threat to an individual in the form of either excessive demands or insufficient

---

[47]   See, for example: Blau, S., & Ellis, A., (2000) *The Albert Ellis Reader: A Guide to Well-Being Using Rational Emotive Behavior Therapy.* Citadel.

[48]   B. F. Skinner, the father of modern behaviorism, has written extensively on the subject since early 1940s. For a typical example of his message, see: Skinner, B. F. (1974). *About Behaviorism.* Knopf.

[49]   For more details, read my book on stress: Dolan, S. L. (2006). *Stress, Self-Esteem, Health and Work.* London: Palgrave Macmillan.

resources. Although most of us are able to respond adequately to stressful situations most of the time, our bodies and minds have a limited capacity to respond to stressors. When we are exposed to too many stressors over a long period, our ability to cope with them diminishes; constant activation of the stress response (and the corresponding secretion of such hormones as adrenalin and noradrenalin) takes a toll on us, physically and mentally.

Specific beliefs and values are activated (or inhibited) when we react to stress. Values associated with high performance—including, among others, friendliness, creativity, achievement, and commitment—tend to be inhibited when we are either under - or overstimulated. Understimulation leads to boredom; overstimulation can lead to hyperactivity, which can result in exhaustion and finally, in what is commonly referred to as "burnout." Both scenarios depress values that play a crucial role in a healthy, fulfilled life.

Although there is a plethora of research on stress, the knowledge gained from all this studying has not sufficiently migrated into our lives or work. The need to develop work and life environments in which stress is manageable is increasingly pressing—as stress levels are rapidly rising. But this requires a major shift that will only occur when we all recognize the conditions that activate stress and understand the serious toll it can take on our lives. Those in positions of influence, such as leaders, parents, and coaches, must be aware that negative levels of stress can impair individuals—and that when this happens, not only people but also (business and other) outcomes will suffer tremendously.

In more-developed countries, an interesting phenomenon has occurred over the past several years. In cultures in which performance has become highly valued and financially rewarded, people shift their behavior trying to become "super-achievers." Although they may have other values, such as family happiness or harmony, these values recede into the background as people focus on those dominant cultural values associated with high achievement. This super-achiever behavior is widely known as Type A behavior. Research shows that Type A individuals tend to create stress for themselves and make already stressful situations worse than they otherwise might be. Furthermore, particular aspects of the Type A personality (specifically anger, hostility, and aggression) may lead to heart attacks. Interestingly, Type A behavior was first described and is continuing to be on the rise in the same countries in which Ray and Anderson are discovering a growing population of Cultural Creatives.

It should be noted that values in and of themselves are neither good nor bad. It is the extent to which an individual expresses a value through behavior that gives the value its negative or positive association in that situation. For example, an individual who values power may demonstrate this value by dominating or controlling others or by relentlessly pursuing financial acquisition, while someone else who values power uses it judiciously to achieve shared organizational goals or to promote a fair and just workplace.

Exhibit 2.2 provides some examples of how typical beliefs and values can lead to harmful behaviors and outcomes (column A) and some examples of how we can alter our beliefs and values to produce positive behaviors and outcomes (column B).

Exhibit 2.2: Beliefs, values, and stress

	COLUMN A negative	COLUMN B positive
BELIEFS	• *Without exception*, we must complete all work within the minimal timeframe. • Work is our first and only priority. • Behavior is either 'right' or 'wrong.' • If you are not aggressive, people will not respect you (you either step over people or they will step on you). • Showing symptoms of stress is a sign of weakness. • Self-esteem is based on success and rewards from work.	• We need to evaluate the situation and achieve the best results within reasonable parameters. • Individuals should seek a balance between energy deployed at work, at home, and for personal needs. • We need to develop flexibility in how we evaluate people and situations. • We need to differentiate assertiveness from aggression and understand how our behavior can create negative or positive outcomes. • Creating healthy boundaries helps us to be physically and psychologically healthy. • Self-esteem is based on a holistic notion of a happy life to include work, relationships and many other aspects that give us joy.
VALUES	• Efficiency • Achievement • Performance • Power • Personal Fortitude • Recognition	• Adaptability • Life Balance • Fairness • Emotional self-control • Wellbeing • Harmony

BEHAVIORS	• Behaviors which predisposes stress and may lead to disease:
	  – Frustration
	  – Perfectionism
	  – Isolation
	  – Anger/Rage
		• Behavior which favors emotional control and promotes wellness:
		  – Pragmatism
		  – Learning
		  – Affiliation
		  – Happiness/satisfaction

OUTCOMES	• Poor physical or mental health • Failing or limited personal relationships • Decreased performance over time	• Sound mental and physical health • Fulfilling relationships • Improved performance over time

SOURCE: Dolan, S. L., Garcia, S., & Richely, B. (2006). *Managing by Values: Corporate Guide to Living, Being Alive and Making a Living in the 21st Century.* London: Palgrave MacMillan. p. 42. Used with authors permission.

2.3 Value formation

Individual values are formed in infancy, childhood, and adolescence based on the models of parents, teachers, friends, and the like. Values are learned, oftentimes unconsciously imbibed, and transmitted. Values are caught and taught. I've been affected, influenced, and changed by the values and virtues of people with whom I've been in contact over the years (see the discussion of my evolution in the introduction). Similarly, my values and virtues have touched other people's lives. Often I receive warm and affectionate messages from former graduate students thanking me for my mentoring, which I take to mean my having taught them the necessary hard skills, such as doing research, but also the soft skills, such as instilling values and enjoying the process of conducting that research—skills that I believe are equally necessary.

In this context we can appreciate yet another definition of values: "the ideals that give significance to our lives, that are reflected in the priorities that we choose, and that we act on consistently and repeatedly." As ideals, values are both tools and goals for social transformation, for the renewal of public life, and for the renewal of community and society.

Values and needs

In the book *Values Shift: A Guide to Personal and Organizational Transformation*,[50] Brian Hall identifies eight stages of value formation. Many of these stages are informed by such popular theories of human motivation and need as those espoused by Maslow.[51] The stages are 1) safety, 2) security, 3) family, 4) institution, 5) vocation, 6) new order, 7) wisdom, and 8) world order in that sequence. Each stage includes core values that serve as both its goals and the means to achieve it. The values in each stage are associated with specific behaviors and can explain subsequent developments of people in and out of organizational life.

Despite the fact that it is old, Maslow's hierarchy of needs is still being used by therapists and coaches today. Maslow claimed that values reflect

---

[50] Hall, B. (1994). *Values Shift: A Guide to Personal and Organizational Transformation*. Twin Lights.

[51] Maslow, A. (1943). A theory of human motivation. *Psychological Review, 50*, 370–396.

a person's judgment and help him or her sort out what is important in life. In other words, needs are already embedded in our values. In his later work, Maslow described what he considered the important values that define an individual's *being*; he called these "Being Values," or "B Values." According to Maslow, people who are self-actualized tend to have incorporated more B Values than those who are at lower levels on the needs hierarchy. The B Values include the following:

- wholeness/unity/oneness

- perfection/just-so-ness

- completion/finality/ending

- justice/fairness

- aliveness/full-functioning

- richness/intricacy

- simplicity/essential/honesty

- beauty/form/richness

- goodness

- uniqueness/idiosyncrasy/novelty

- effortlessness/ease/perfect

- playfulness/joy/humor

- truth/reality/beauty/pure

- self-sufficiency/independence

Value formation, the evolution or purposeful development of values, manifests itself in personal renewal (for the individual) and social transformation (for the collective). Renewal and transformation require going beyond the survival phase of life, which is focused simply on securing one's safety. Because all phases of life have corresponding values, which act as both goals and means, moving from one stage to another requires modifying values.

The value shift from personal survival to living with a sense of belonging to a family or an institution includes accepting their goals-values and means-values. Further transformation or renewal would mean entering a still higher phase of life, preparing for and dedicating oneself to one's life work (calling, vocation, or profession) in view of constructing or renewing the social order. This again requires discovering new goals and purposes in life and in conjunction, forming new values. For the next level of renewal and transformation, one must learn and embrace the value of interdependence, which makes possible productive and fulfilling relationships between people on a global scale. In this stage, values of prophetic wisdom and world order are acquired and developed.

Some people believe that understanding needs is more important than understanding values, because, they claim, needs are more likely to explain behavior than values. No doubt we all have needs. Also there is no doubt that basic needs have to be satisfied regardless of our values. We need to breathe fresh air, and unless we continue to breathe, we will die. No matter how much we value a healthy ecosystem and fresh air, if our immediate survival needs are so profound that satisfying them requires all our energy, those survival needs will explain our behavior more than our values will. In a couple of popular films, people survived an airplane crash by eating the flesh of their dead buddies. As terrible as this may sound, their actions fulfilled survival needs. I am convinced, however, that in all situations where survival is not at stake, values are by far more important than needs.

This is because our values help us make choices about what to commit to. If you commit time and energy to something that violates one of your core values, you will eventually feel resentful or frustrated. This may start with a niggling in the back of your mind, telling you that something is not right. If you persist in choosing activities and relationships that don't honor your values, you will develop a full-blown and persistent sense that something is terribly wrong. Your values are the qualities that define you; they are at the core of who you are. Without them, you would not be you.

Think of a time when life was rich, fulfilling, exhilarating, flowing. Maybe there were some challenges, but you were on a roll. It may have been minutes, hours, or weeks; the length of time doesn't matter. What was important was the experience itself, but what about that experience made it so powerful? What values were you honoring?

Now, think about things that drive you nuts, make you angry, or leave you frustrated. Examine each of these, and I'm certain you'll discover that a value dear to you is being violated. What value is being neglected or stepped on in these situations?

After these two quick self-reflections, consider what it is that you can't live with and still be true to yourself? What is so much a part of you that you haven't thought to put it on the list yet?

Value formation in an organization

Some specific factors influence the formation of values in an organization. Of the many variables that we can identify, the following seem to be the most important:

The beliefs and values of the founders: Every company starts its life as an impulse from an idea, and within this burgeoning enterprise, some principles are more or less implicit. To implement their idea, the founders assemble the necessary financial, human, and material resources. These founders, in general, determine how the company is defined, how it resolves its problems, and how it adapts externally and integrates internally. The founders not only possesses a high degree of determination and self-confidence but also usually have very firm ideas about how the world works, the roles that different people can play, how to arrive at "the truth," and how to exert control over time and space. The ideas and principles of the founding group tend to be dissipated over time as the company grows, unless special efforts are made to encourage their continuation. Many companies that exhibit an especially strong cultural identity have managed to maintain a coherence and strength of values inherited from their founders.

The beliefs and values of the current management and the system of rewards: At any given time, the management of a company can decide to perpetuate, revitalize, or even radically modify the beliefs and values of the founders. One of their tasks is to manage the perennial conflict between the traditional and the modern in all aspects of an enterprise's operations. This is also one of the basic problems underlying generational succession in companies.

One of the strongest formative influences on beliefs and values in employees is the existing mechanism of compensation. For example, it is pointless for management to make speeches about the importance of innovation if they do not stimulate and compensate creative efforts.

Training and the influence of coaches: An essential mechanism for modifying beliefs and values is training. Earlier I mentioned that changing values and behaviors required "unlearning" beliefs, and in keeping with this, true learning consists of unlearning irrelevant beliefs and replacing them with new ones. Such training may take the form of attending courses, reading suitable publications (such as this book, I hope), or interacting with coaches. As well as inculcating new values, it is often important for a company to focus on values that have previously been learned and partially forgotten. Senior managers with professional training can be very effective in reactivating these, helping to ensure continuity throughout the lifespan of an organization. Clearly it would be unrealistic to think of promoting values like honesty and initiative through attendance at seminars. Competent, professional business coaches can also play a major role here.

Legislation: Legislation covering employment, the environment, taxation, and the like in each country significantly influences the beliefs and values in companies.

The "rules of the game" in particular markets: The degree of free competition in any market, as well as accepted conventions or customs, imposes certain rules of the game that condition the beliefs and values of companies. Among the beliefs most strengthened by competitive pressure is that it is important to beat your rivals and gain short-term advantage or benefit, using any means necessary to achieve this regardless of the long-term effect on the viability of the business or society.

The prevailing social values of the period: At the beginning of the twentieth century, the predominant social values in the developed countries were different from those now, which in turn will be different in the future. For example, transparency is a relatively emergent value; previously confidentiality was of the utmost importance. And employees are now referred to as "organizational members," whereas in earlier times they were considered merely cogs in the metaphorical organizational machine.

The cultural tradition of each society: In every society, the social values and business values influence each other mutually. A large part of the economic success of Japan was due to its urge to show the Western world its collective strength, which was achieved by the incorporation of its traditional social values—such as the drive for continuous improvement, harmony, loyalty, and pride in belonging to a family or group—into its industrial arena.

The history of success and failure of the company: Lastly, it must be stated that the systems of beliefs and values of the company are self-sustaining if its results are considered good. If a company does well profit-wise and explicitly includes values such as dealing honestly with its customers in its systems, then it will tend to perpetuate that value as essential for its business. This is the "winning formula" factor. In contrast, if this company builds up losses, it is likely or at least possible that it will reconsider its system of values.

Hierarchy of values: The value of values

At the root of my thinking about values—derived from my own experience and validated in my work over decades and across continents—is that your *hierarchy of your values* will determine what you do and how you live your life. It is almost impossible to align all your values at the same time with your goals. And the attempt to do so can be so overwhelming that you may give up. But you can make significant progress to a healthier and more fulfilling life by identifying your core values, putting them in an order, and choosing a strategy for aligning those at the top of the list with your goals. This synchronization of your values and goals will be effective as long as your values hierarchy does not change, and in reality the hierarchy is dynamic and may change.

Claims in such best-selling books as *The Secret*[52] that by using positive energy and focusing on aligning several values, one can attain all life goals simultaneously are utopian. And not only are such messages chimerical, but misleading readers with claims that positive thinking can effect real-world outcomes can actually be very dangerous. The "secret" offers false hope to those in true need of more-conventional coaching.

So, how do we organize our values? What are the criteria for the hierarchy? The truth is that there are no rules, and each person's hierarchy is unique. Philosophers, theologians, and other thinkers have, however, wrestled with this for millennia, with some arguing that certain values are absolute or that there are criteria for prioritizing values or determining the value of specific values that hold true across time and place. In "A Study on the Hierarchy of Values," Tong-Keun Min, a Korean scholar steeped in a combined Asian and European philosophies, offers some principles identified by M. Scheler (1874–1928) that are useful in ranking values:[53]

- **Timelessness:** The longer the value lasts, the higher it is. For example, while the value of pleasure lasts for the duration of the feeling of pleasure, the mental value remains after the disappearance of the circumstances.

- **Indivisibility:** The harder it is to reduce the quality of the value as its carrier divides or the harder it is to increase the quality of the value as its carrier enlarges, the higher the value is. For example, while the value of material goods reduces as the goods divide, the

---

[52]   Byrne, R. (2006). *The Secret*. Atria Books.

[53]   Tong-Keun Min. (1998, Aug. 10–15). *A Study on the Hierarchy of Values*. Paper presented at the Twentieth World Congress of Philosophy. http://www.bu.edu/wcp/Papers/Valu/ValuMin.htm.

value of mental goods is indivisible and not related to the number of people concerned.

- **Independence:** The higher value becomes the base for the lower value. The fewer other values the value has as its base, the higher it is.

- **Depth of satisfaction:** There is an intrinsic relationship between the rank of the value and the depth of satisfaction from its realization. In other words, the deeper the satisfaction connected to the value is, the higher the value is. For example, the physical satisfaction is strong but shallow. On the contrary, the satisfaction from artistic meditation is a deep experience. The depth of satisfaction is not related to its strength

- **Absoluteness:** The less the sense of the value is related to the existence of its carrier, the higher the value is. For example, the value of pleasure has significance in relation to the sense of sensuality. The value of life exists for those with the sense of life, but the moral value exists absolutely and independently from those who feel it.

The more we explore values and try to deal with them in our lives and work, the more complex the subject becomes. Although many associate the word *value* with economics (and we saw earlier in this chapter that there is an economic dimension to value), value is not the same as price. In fact, the value of a thing or service is often not truly reflected in its price. The price of a thing is its exchange value, which varies from time to time, from place to place, from people to people; it is always changeable and changing. Not attributing a price to something, or making it available at a low price, does not necessarily mean that it has no value or limited value. For example, we do not put a price on air, but it is very valuable to us. Tap water is cheap, but water is essential to human life and has almost boundless value. Land, the sun, and light also have boundless and essential value for humans, animals, and plants. A nurturing and caring spouse or mother is another example. We can not measure nurturing and caring as values, but we know how essential they are to present and future happiness. Air pollution, water pollution, the destruction of the ecosystem, and loss of nurturing and caring are, conversely, grave anti-values that threaten the existence of humans and other living organisms.

Most of us will agree that we hold a set of principles to be important, that we value integrity, and accountability, freedom, and respect for others. Most organizations will describe their values as including care for the customer, safety of their employees, innovation, and performance. But it is idealistic to believe that every action can fulfill all of these, and the test of "walking the talk" has become a cliché. Most employees in the vast majority of organizations will say that what is written on the wall (or published on the company's website) is far from reality. It is not that companies do not believe in these principles, it is simply impossible to achieve them all. A company, like a person, has to choose, and in these choices reveals its true values hierarchy. A hierarchy of values is seen most clearly when there are limited resources and choices have to be made regarding how they will be applied. These choices become symbols of what is really valued.

Creating a hierarchy of values is not a simple task. In the next section, I will present a method and a logic to help you develop your hierarchy of values. I will introduce you to the tri-axial model, which allows you to classify all your important values on three axes (dimensions) and then explore the relative dominance (meaning) of each axis. This method is very flexible: You generate the axes from your individual values, but as you continue to work with it, you refine and rethink those. By the end of the process, you may not have the same values in the model as you had when you began. The anchor is the axis; the relevant importance of specific values and the hierarchy will come later in the process. Let us begin by understanding the logic for the tri-axial model.

2.4 Modeling the universe of values: The 3Es tri-axial approach

What are your core values? What are the core values of your corporation? What are the core values of your family? Your community? Your country? Which values of yours would you select and place in a hierarchy that will become a guide for your actions, a guide for behavior? Why—or under what circumstances—would you be prepared to adjust your values, and your hierarchy, to create a better fit with your mate, family, work, and the like? Which values are you not prepared to modify? What is the best way to discover whether your core values are being supported or undermined by your work or family?

While grappling with these questions, my colleagues and I developed a model that can describe any universe of values. We call it the **3Es tri-axial model of values.**[54] Exhibit 2.3 encapsulates the primary elements of this model, and exhibit 2.4 is an example of a tri-axial structure in use. The tri-axial framework is flexible; one can use it to detect or uncover values, to categorize values, to clarify and prioritize values, and to help align values. The beauty of this model is not necessarily its completeness but rather its simplicity (parsimony) and applicability to various individuals, corporations, and communities. In this section, I will familiarize you with the basic structure of the model.

The underlying assumption of the 3Es tri-axial model is that values can be detected in all universes (personal, family, organization, community) regardless of their nature, mission, or vision and once identified, they can be classified according to three core dimensions or axes: **economic-pragmatic axis, ethical-social axis,** and **emotional-developmental axis (the 3Es).** Also foundational to this model is the assumption that all personal and organizational values are situated in one of these dimensions. (We refer to the 3Es tri-axial model, for short, as either "3Es model" or "tri-axial model.")

These axes were identified and the model developed through both classical research and primary empirical research; I tested it and refined it in hundreds of workshops and seminars across the globe (different countries, different cultures, different sectors, and different categories of employees). The reaction of the participants was overwhelming.[55]

---

[54] See: Dolan, S. L., Garcia, S., & Richley, B. (2006). *Managing by Values: Corporate Guide to Living, Being Alive and Making a Living in the 21st Century.* London: Palgrave Macmillan.

[55] Currently, my colleagues and I are conducting a 30-country validation study—VAC (Values Across Cultures)—about the meaning of values. This project focuses on public sector employees in 30 countries across the globe.

Exhibit 2.3: The 3Es tri-axial model of values

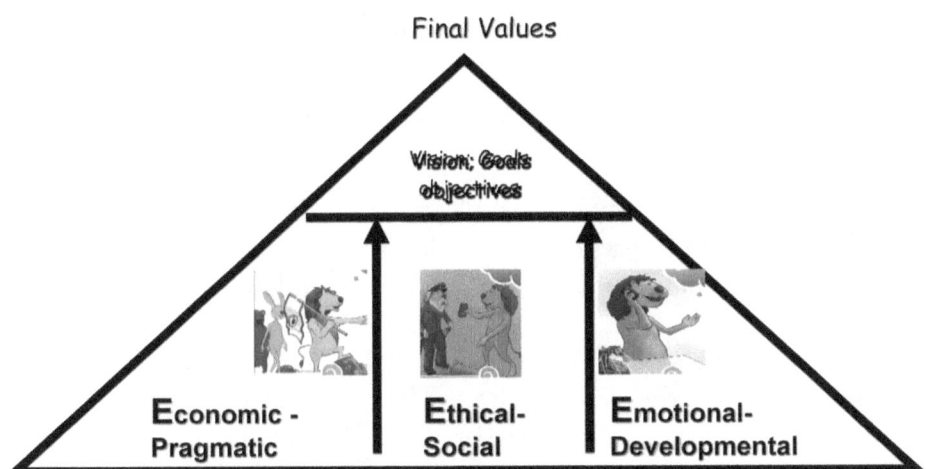

The model borrows some ideas developed in the 1970s by Milton Rockeach, who divided individual values into **terminal/final values,** which are desirable end-states of existence (e.g., happiness, wisdom), and **instrumental values,** which are desirable modes of behavior (e.g., acting honestly, earning lots of money). A functional relationship exists between these two: Instrumental values describe behaviors that facilitate the attainment of terminal values (and instrumental values can be detected and categorized using the 3Es model). The former have received more attention in the literature than the latter and are more widely used by researchers and practitioners to describe an organization's culture.

Let us start by observing the simplest and most fundamental organization that we all know, the family. Think about your family or others with whom you are familiar. Most of us know intuitively that if a family is to be successful as a unit, a balance must exist between the axes that are shared by the couple. Most of us also know that the family (and marriage, more specifically) in the twenty-first century is in crisis: Rates of divorce and separation are alarming; violence within the family is growing; and a general sense of uneasiness and marital dissatisfaction is on the rise. Why is this happening?

A family, like any other organization, has objectives (final values). If these are not shared by the couple, and if the couple's instrumental values—which can be plotted along the three axes—are not aligned with their final values, the family is doom to fail. Thus, agreement on the final values alone will not ensure success. The family will likely fail if even one of following exists:

- There is discordance between the couple's economic-pragmatic values

- The couple's ethical-social values are not in sync

- One or both parties loses passion for the relationship (the most critical emotional-developmental value binding the couple)

If we think about families and close-knit groups of friends as living organizations that struggle to survive and be happy in a complex world, we can see that challenges confronted by larger organizations such as corporations and governmental bodies are far greater. The same shared values necessary for positive sustainable relationships in the family and among friends are critical in the workplace. It follows then that assessing an organizational culture by identifying core values, the level of which they are shared, and the extent to which they are congruent with organizational members' personal values is very important. The CBV methodology, which I'll present in depth in the following chapters, enables us to plot these values around these three axes.

Exhibit 2.4: An organizational tri-axial model and possible outcomes of value alignment

Exhibit 2.4 shows a 3Es model and certain values associated with each axis. It also shows the following relationships or linkages between the axes and outcomes of these congruencies:

- Congruency between the emotional-developmental axis and the economic-pragmatic axis leads to greater innovation

- Congruency between the economic-pragmatic axis and the ethical-social axis leads to enhancement of survival

- Congruency between the ethical-social axis and the emotional-developmental axis increases sensitivity and makes the organization more socially responsible

The following examples illustrate these linkages:

- **Survival** (economic-pragmatic values and ethical-social values): A company that is involved in unethical behavior (e.g., practicing gymnastics with the accounting or participating in fraud) will certainly not survive. Likewise, a husband cheating on his wife, or vice versa, endangers the survival of the couple as a unit.

- **Innovativeness** (emotional-developmental values and economic-pragmatic values): The best innovations are born of people's positive passion. There are hundreds of examples to illustrate this. Take the invention of Post-it Notes. Art Fry, a 3M new-product-development researcher, created the sticky yellow notes as a substitute for scrap paper bookmarks that kept falling out of his church choir hymnal. Frustrated with his bookmarks, he remembered a strange weak adhesive a 3M scientist had developed while searching for its opposite, a super-strong glue. Fry put the accidental adhesive to use. His persistent curiosity coupled with personal desire led him to invent a product that revolutionized office work and research.

- **Sensitivity** (ethical-social and emotional-developmental values). You don't need to wait for legislation requiring you to separate your garbage for recycling. If you are concerned about the environment, you can take the time and make the effort to separate your household (and workplace) trash and recycle it regardless of the need for legal compliance. You will do it because of your sensitivity. In the same vein, you will not smoke in places where you think it may bother others, even when smoking is permitted.

Pages and pages of examples exist. Why don't you try this simple exercise: Identify the crossing of values that enhance your survival, sensitivity, and moments of innovation by identifying the interface of relevant values.

CBV Reflection ♣ ♠ ♥

Values Intersection Exercise

Think of a family context, a work context, or a community context. Complete the following sentences:

*I am more **sensitive** to my Family/Team/Community (circle only one) because of the interaction of my following core values:*

_____

_____

*I am more **innovative** within the context of my Family/Team/Community (circle only one) because of the interaction my following core values:*

_____

_____

*I am know that I am adding to the **survival of** my Family/Team/ Community (circle only one) because of the interaction my following core values:*

_____

_____

_____

Here I need to add a very important note that will be critical later. Although exhibit 2.4 presents a perfectly symmetrical triangle, most triangles developed using the tri-axial model are not symmetrical and need not be symmetrical. Moreover, although the symmetry of exhibit 2.4 may imply that all three axes have equal importance in one's hierarchy of values, this is certainly not the case in the vast majority of such hierarchies. For the purpose of this introduction, I used an equilateral triangle almost metaphorically, to emphasize that the aggregate of the three axes is the universe of values that represents the world being examined. In chapter 4, I will show you how to draw an actual triangle based on your values and the axes into which they fall.

2.5 Values and culture

Every culture has a set of moral and social values. These derive from its prehistory and are modified with each generation. Some cultures or societies change faster than others, but there is a stability found in a common set of values. These values, true enough, are often held as ideals more than implemented as realities. Still, the accepted set of values, ideals, goals, and standards are part of the character of a culture. It is a basic goal of every community, tribe, and nation to maintain its own identity as a group. The specific values found in a culture relate to this maintenance. There are numerous disciplines that define the common aspects of values found in all human societies. These have been developed by sociologists and anthropologists in great detail. In this section, I will try to provide a brief overview of some common characteristics and the roles of values in the following levels of culture: organizational culture, family culture, community and national culture. These are the principal levels of interventions for coaches, so I thought some additional information might be instrumental.

Best-selling author Riane Eisler has developed two extraordinary models—domination and partnership—that can be used to view any culture. She claims that every system falls somewhere along the continuum between the two models; no culture is purely one or the other. Eisler also identifies values connected to each model and shows how these affect every relationship in our lives: parents and children, women and men, government and citizens, humans and nature. She focuses on seven key relationships and has developed key practices for strengthening them:

First, our relationship with ourselves; second, national community; fifth, international and multicultural relationships; sixth, our relationship with nature and the living environment; and seventh, our spiritual relations.[56]

Values and organizational culture

Basically, organizational culture is the personality of the organization, but it is not often easy to put your finger on it.[57] Culture is composed of the assumptions, values, norms, and tangible signs (artifacts) of the principal stakeholders of an organization and their behaviors. It is difficult to express or describe, but everyone recognizes a culture when they experience it. Members of an organization, for instance, soon come to sense the organization's unique culture even if they can not articulate it, which is often the case. Certain broad types of cultures are quite distinct: The culture of a large, for-profit corporation is different from that of a hospital which is different from that of a university. You can tell the culture of an organization by the arrangement of furniture, what employees brag about, what members wear, and the like, in the same way you can get a feeling about someone's personality by being attentive to his or her language, tone of voice, and appearance. But cultural recognition is one thing, understanding it on a deep level is another.

Corporate culture can be looked at as a system. Inputs include feedback from, say, society, professions, laws, stories, heroes, values placed on traits such as competition or service, and so on. The process is based on assumptions, values and norms, such as values on money, time, facilities, space and people. Outputs include, organizational behaviors, technologies, strategies, image, products, services, and appearance, among others.

The concept of culture is particularly important when attempting to manage organization-wide change. Coaches and organizational consultants are coming to realize that despite the best-laid plans, if an organizational change initiative does not focus on modifying corporate culture as well as changing structures and processes, it will not succeed.

---

[56] For more, see: Eisler, R. (2002). *The Power of Partnership: Seven Relationships That Will Change Your Life.* New World Library.

[57] For more, see my discussion of culture reengineering in chapter 4.

A great deal of literature has been generated over the past decade about the concept of organizational culture, particularly about how to change it. An overwhelming majority of organizational change efforts fail. Usually, this failure is credited to lack of understanding about the strong role of culture and the role it plays in organizations. Because of this, many strategic planners now place as much emphasis on identifying strategic values as they do on an enterprise's espoused mission and vision.

An organization in which staff respond to stimulus because of their alignment with organizational values is considered to have a "strong" culture. Conversely, if there is little alignment between staff and organizational values and management must rely on extensive procedures and bureaucracy to maintain control, the culture is considered "weak." When the culture is strong, people do things because they believe they are the right thing to do. This type of culture develops, for example, when there is a strong reliance on a central charismatic figure in the organization or an evangelical belief in the organization's values. It can also arise when a friendly climate is at the base of the company.

Edgar Schein, an MIT Sloan School of Management professor who has written extensively about organizational culture,[58] defines organizational culture as "the residue of success" within an organization. and claims that it is more resistant to change than any other element of the organization—products, services, founders' beliefs, and leadership. His organizational model described from the standpoint of the observer, contains three cognitive levels of organizational culture:

- The first and most cursory level refers to the organizational attributes that can be seen, felt and heard by the uninitiated observer. Included are the facilities, offices, furnishings, visible awards and recognition, the way that its members dress, and how each person visibly interacts with each other and with organizational outsiders.

- The next level deals with the professed culture of an organization's members. At this level, company slogans, mission statements and other operational creeds are often expressed, and local and personal

---

[58] Schein, E. H. (2005). *Organizational Culture and Leadership* (3rd ed.). Jossey-Bass. First edition was published in 1985.

values are widely expressed within the organization. Organizational behavior at this level usually can be studied by interviewing the organization's membership and using questionnaires to gather attitudes about organizational membership.

• At the third and deepest level, the organization's tacit assumptions are found. These are the elements of culture that are unseen and not cognitively identified in everyday interactions between organizational members. Additionally, these are the elements of culture which are often taboo to discuss inside the organization. Many of these 'unspoken rules' exist without the conscious knowledge of the membership. Those with sufficient experience to understand this deepest level of organizational culture usually become acclimatized to its attributes over time, thus reinforcing the invisibility of their existence. Surveys and casual interviews with organizational members cannot draw out these attributes—rather much more in-depth means is required to first identify then understand organizational culture at this level. Notably, culture at this level is the underlying and driving element often missed by organizational behaviorists.

Schein's model not only gives us a way to begin to understand paradoxical behaviors in organizations—behaviors that seem to be out of synch with the organization's espoused mission and vision statement—it also constitutes an argument for formulating new methods of attempting to effect change in organizations based on a more profound understanding of culture than those often crafted by traditional organizational change agents. (We will discuss this more in chapter 4.) Furthermore, his model may begin to give us a way to look at the importance of the relationships between people in the organization, including the way in which they are "managed."

Studies confirm that the way people are managed and developed delivers a higher return on investment than new technology, R&D, competitive strategy, or quality initiatives. In addition, culture that emphasizes employee effectiveness is linked to shareholder returns. It is no wonder that many CEOs use the now-clichéd phrase: "The most important asset of our organization is our people." The broader implications of this are obvious for corporate contenders striving to enhance value through quality and customer-centricity in an increasingly complex, professionally demanding, and continuously changing global market.

The system of beliefs and values that shaped the Western management and organizational model at the beginning of the twentieth century is impotent in the new business paradigm. Rigid management models based on hierarchical control of employees under conditions of relative stability externally and internally are a shaky foundation for companies in today's global turmoil and rapid technological change. Traditional command-and-control management practices stifle the sparks of creativity critical to innovation in and adaptation to a diverse environment and essential to the ability to successfully compete in that environment. The changes of the twenty-first century have fueled the drive for a fundamental rethinking of organizational structure and operating philosophy, toward a renewal of corporate culture. Values are now understood to be the essence, the DNA, of corporate culture and shared values are vital to the robust versatility required for success in today's global market.

Stability must be created from within an organization and be embedded in a culture that preserves the best of its past and simultaneously fosters new ways of thinking and doing. While just about everyone agrees with this in theory, putting it into practice is another matter. Determining which values and beliefs to change, how and when to initiate the change process, how far to take it, and most important, how to lead and steer cultural reengineering without complete collapse presents at the very least major stumbling blocks. The Coaching by Values process addresses these issues and provides specific tools for keeping a change process on course and on target.

Since my colleagues and I first articulated our ideas about the significance of values to corporate leaders and organizational change agents in our 1997 book *Managing by Values*,[59] we have seen wonderful successes that have helped us refine the Coaching by Values process. In a 2010 *Harvard Business Review* blog, Rosabeth Moss Kanter summarized the logic behind such a values-based change process and suggested specific

---

[59] Garcia, S., & Dolan, S. L. (1997). *Dirección por Valores*. Madrid: McGraw-Hill; Dolan, S. L., Garcia, S., & Richley, B. (2006). *Managing by Values: Corporate Guide to Living, Being Alive and Making a Living in the 21ˢᵗ Century*. London: Palgrave Macmillan.

ways leaders can strengthen their companies by keeping values front and center: [60]

1. Values should be a priority for leaders; they should be invoked in their messages and on the agenda for management discussions.

2. The entire work force should enter the conversation; employees should be invited to discuss or interpret values and principles in conjunction with their peers, who help ensure alignment.

3. Principles should be codified, made explicit, transmitted in writing in many media, and reviewed regularly to make sure people understand and remember them.

4. Statements about values and principles invoke a higher purpose, a purpose beyond current tasks that indicates service to society. This purpose should become part of the company's brand and a source of competitive differentiation.

5. The words should become a basis for on-going dialogue that guides debate when there is controversy or initial disagreement. Decisions should be supported by reference to particular values or principles.

6. Values should guide choices, in terms of business opportunities to pursue or reject, or in terms of investments with a longer time horizon that might seem uneconomic today.

7. As they become internalized by employees, values and principles should substitute for more impersonal or coercive rules. They should serve as a control system against violations, excesses, or veering off course.

8. Actions reflecting values and principles—especially difficult choices—become the basis for iconic stories that are easy to

---

[60] Kanter, R. M. (2010, June 14). Ten Essentials for Getting Value from Values, *Harvard Business Review* blog. *http://blogs.hbr.org/kanter/2010/06/ten-essentials-for-getting-val.html*.

remember and retell, reinforcing to employees and the world what the company stands for, the company branding.

9. Values are aspirational; they signal long-term intentions that guide thinking about the future.

10. Principles, purpose, and values should also be discussed with other stakeholders: suppliers, distributors, and other business partners, to promote consistent high standards everywhere.

My Personal Experience with Value-Driven Leadership

Michele Hunt

I have been a student and a teacher of values-driven leadership all my life. My life has been a journey of discovering, witnessing (and being a part of) the extraordinary things values-driven leaders have accomplished in their organizations, communities, and personal lives.

Values powerfully and beautifully shaped my life

My life was conceived and nurtured by the two greatest people I have ever met. My parents gave me the gift of witnessing the "value of values." My parents came from very challenging beginnings. My father was the second oldest of 12 children. They lived in extreme poverty in the inner city of Detroit, Michigan. His passion was the arts; he was gifted with a beautiful, classical baritone voice. He also played every wind instrument. In spite of his many talents, his mother told him that his dreams of singing and performing around the world were unrealistic. My mother lost her mother at the young age of seven, and her father deserted her and her siblings. They were moved four times to different homes by the time she was 10. Life was hard; my mother even suffered abuse, but she escaped through books. She journeyed around the world through the stories she read, imagining she was in exotic places. Her most cherished dream was to have a family and give them the love and support she had missed as a child.

Despite their beginnings, when my parents married, they consciously and deliberately envisioned the family and the life they wanted to create together, and they committed to a set of nonnegotiable values with which to guide their decisions and actions. My parents succeeded in making their hopes and dreams come true. Dad sang and performed all over the world. He produced elaborate USO shows with audiences of more than 10,000 people. My mom's vision of a family bonded by love also came true. She was at the heart of the creation of love, beauty, and joy in our home. Her family is the center of her life, and to this day we are extraordinarily close. Her vision of traveling to exotic places was also fulfilled; we lived in Alaska, Arizona, Kentucky, and the country of Panama. I experienced in a very personal way "the value of values:

Values were the magic of Herman Miller

I served on the executive leadership team as Vice President for People at Herman Miller. Under the leadership of Max De Pree, I saw how the power of shared values transformed this Fortune 500 company from near failure into Fortune's Most Admired Company in the World. We learned the hard way that nothing fails like success.

After decades of success, we had started becoming irrelevant. We had become complacent and insulated and had developed a touch of arrogance. Most damaging, we had failed to pass on the company values—the secret sauce of our 60 years of success. When we were small, we could share the values through stories and relationships, but we had become large, complex, and impersonal. The consequences would have been dire had we not changed. Max called for a companywide renewal. We renewed our mission and created a shared vision. We accomplished this is a unique manner. We created a disciplined process that authentically engaged every work team and every individual in the company. All the employees wanted the same thing—to reclaim our leadership, "to be a reference point for quality and excellence."

Max insightfully understood that a vision without values is empty and potentially dangerous, so he asked a very important question, "What values do we need to embrace and build into the organization to become a reference point for quality and excellence?"

Once again we went to the people. After hearing their input, we settled on seven core values that would guide everyone's decisions and behaviors:

1. **Customer-focused vision:** Put the customer at the center of our vision.

2. **Participation and teamwork:** Recognize the value and collective genius of people. People have the right and responsibility to contribute their gifts.

3. **Ownership:** Treat employees like owners. Allow everyone to be responsible and accountable for the decisions that affect their work.

4. **Uniqueness:** Encourage people to bring their whole self to work and to contribute their uniqueness to help achieve the company's goals.

5. **Family social and environmental responsibility:** Work, family, community, and the environment are inextricably connected, and our actions had to respect that connection.

6. **Become a learning organization:** Continual learning was a shared commitment.

7. **Financial soundness:** This is essential, but it is not the single aim of our work. It is the result of our commitment to our vision, values, and goals.

The results were amazing! Within 18 months, Herman Miller became

- Fortune's Most Admired Company
- Best Products by Business Week
- One of the 10 Best Companies to Work For
- Best Company for Women
- Best Company for Working Mothers
- Winner of numerous environmental awards
- Recipient of the White House Presidential Citation for environmental responsibility.
- The Best Managed Company in the world (from the Bertelsmann Foundation)

In addition, sales increased 20%, and we returned to double-digit growth.

Values-based coaching

For the past 16 years, my method of coaching has been to help leaders to mobilize their people around a compelling shared vision born of their deeply held shared values, engaging their people in transforming their vision, values, and goals into reality. The results have consistently been outstanding. Two of the companies were invited into Fortune's 100 Best Companies to Work For after engaging in this process. This is the same methodology we used at Herman Miller; it transcends time, cultures, and sectors. The secret to success is a commitment to the organization's shared values. When leaders connect the hearts of people through values to accomplish shared goals amazing things happen.

Michele Hunt is a transformation catalyst and "thinking partner" on cultural transformation and leadership development for leaders around the world. She is a speaker and the author of *DreamMakers: Putting Vision & Values To Work* and *DreamMakers: Agents of Transformation.* She contributed chapters to Peter Senge's *Fifth Discipline FieldBook* and Robert Rosen's *Healthy Companies.* Michele  served in President Bill Clinton's administration as director of the Federal Quality Institute, as a part of the Reinventing Government Initiative. She served on the senior leadership team of Herman Miller as corporate Vice President for People.

Values and culture: The family

In this section, I will try to illustrate the relationships between values and family functioning. To begin with, the meaning of "family values" is vague, but most often associated with social and religious contexts. Its meaning varies as a function of time and national culture. In the United States, for example, from the middle to the end of the twentieth century, the term "family values" (at least as it was bandied about in political debates and the media) referred to fundamentalist Christian values that included a number of specific rigid principles requiring followers to hew to certain behaviors within narrow bounds. But twenty-first-century surveys show a shift in the definition toward the broader principles of "loving, taking care of, and supporting family members." Surveys in the United States also noted that 93% of women thought society should value all types of families.

The more conservative formulation of family values includes valuing "traditional marriage" and a traditional role for women while opposing sex outside conventional marriage. Social and religious conservatives often use the term to promote conservative ideology that supports traditional morality or "Christian" values. American Christians often see their religion as the source of morality and consider the nuclear family to be the essential element in society.

Liberals, on the other hand, have used the phrase to support family planning, affordable child care, and maternity leave as well as equal roles for men and women in raising children and undertaking work outside the home (paid jobs) or within the family (unpaid jobs). According to Riane Eisler, the essence of the family relationship is changing in the developed Western world as the domination of the male is gradually decreasing and more females are establishing collaborative agreements with their male spouses regarding partnership and care.[61]

Confucianism exerts a strong influence on the family culture and values in China and other Asian societies. In Confucian thought, family values, familial relationships, ancestor worship, and filial piety are the primary basis of the philosophical system and are considered virtues to be cultivated. Filial piety is the highest virtue in Chinese culture. The term *filial*—meaning "of a child"—denotes the respect and obedience that a child, originally a son, should show his parents, especially his father. This relationship has been extended by analogy to a series of five cardinal relationships: ruler and subject, father and son, husband and wife, elder and younger brother, and friend and friend. These values are manifest in many aspects of Chinese culture even to this day. Examples are extensive filial responsibilities children have to parents and elders and the profound and enduring concern of parents for their children.

---

[61] In *The Chalice and the Blade* (1988, HarperOne), Eisler traces the powerful effects of everyday exposure to a dominator and shows the difference between those and the effects of the partnership model in every area of life.

Some communities separated by great distances manifest similar views of the family and stress the strength of one's commitment to it throughout life. Hispanics and many Arabs, for instance, value the family above all else; they prize family relationships more than any other communities. When they are growing up, young Hispanics and many young Arabs do not envision their future as a life outside the family unit, and in fact they remain intimately connected to their birth family for the rest of their lives. Children grow up hanging out with their brothers, sisters, and cousins. Parents care for their children, provide for them, and protect them. This acceptance and love, in turn, engenders more of the same. Individuals who grow up in such families develop and exhibit the same love and acceptance for their parents and for other children in the family. This bonding continues through adulthood and into old age. Some sociologists cite it, together with mutual assistance, as the reason there was not a revolution in Spain when unemployment soared to record heights in 2010 and 2011 (over 20% for adults and over 27% for people under 25). Most economists say that when unemployment hits these numbers a social revolution follows, which does not seem to be the case in Spain.

Exhibit 2.5 summarizes the hierarchy of values I've seen in some societies based on general value characteristics in these communities. I don't mean to suggest that every member of these communities holds these values or prioritizes them in this way—in fact, they certainly don't. Nor do I mean to stereotype these cultures or present the value systems with any judgment.

Exhibit 2.5 Comparative hierarchies of values in families

Anglo-Saxon	**Hispanic (& many Arabs)**	**Asian**
Freedom	Family security	Belonging
Independence	Harmony	Respect
Self-reliance	Parental guidance	Harmony
Equality	Age respect	Age respect
Individualism	Authority	Group
Competition	Compromise	Collaboration
Efficiency	Devotion	Quality

Values, community, and national culture: A brief description

Although there are numerous ways of looking at the national and community levels of culture, given the limited scope of this book, let us consider the ideas of one seminal figure in the field of national culture whose pioneering work has greatly influenced the current conversation. Geert Hofstede, a Dutch organizational sociologist, has studied the interactions between national cultures and organizational cultures. He argues that there are national and regional cultural groupings that affect the behavior of organizations, and that these are persistent across time. By and large Hofstede and his colleagues have shown that these cultures affect the behavior of individuals.[62] As editor-in-chief of *Cross Cultural Management—An International Journal*, I invited Hofstede and a colleague to reflect on the evolution of his pioneer work.[63]

They identified five characteristics that define a culture and influence organizational and personal behavior:

- **Power distance** is the degree to which a society expects there to be power differences among people. A high score reflects the belief that some individuals should wield more power than others. A low score reflects the view that all people should have equal rights.

- **Uncertainty avoidance** is the extent to which a society accepts uncertainty and risk.

- **Individualism vs. collectivism** is the extent to which people are expected to stand up for themselves or to act as a member of a group or organization.

---

[62]   See: Hofstede, G. (2001). *Culture's Consequences: Comparing Values, Behaviors, Institutions, and Organizations Across Nations* (2nd ed.). Sage; Hofstede, G., & Hofstede, G. J. (2005). *Cultures and Organizations: Software of the Mind* (Revised and expanded 2nd ed.). McGraw-Hill.

[63]   Minkov, M. (with Hofstede, G.). (2011). The evolution of Hofstede's Doctrine. *Cross Cultural Management—An International Journal, 18*(1), 10-20.

- **Masculinity vs. femininity** is the importance a society places on traditionally male and female values. Male values, for example, include competitiveness, assertiveness, ambition, and the accumulation of wealth and material possessions.

- **Long-term vs. short-term orientation** describes a society's "time horizon," or the importance attached to the future as opposed to the past and present. In long-term-oriented societies, thrift and perseverance are valued highly; in short-term-oriented societies, respect for tradition and reciprocation of gifts and favors are valued more. A high score indicates a long-term orientation. Eastern nations tend to score especially high here, with Western nations scoring low and the less-developed nations very low; China scored highest and Pakistan lowest.

Hofstede's doctrine has generated controversies; it has been both undervalued and overused. His conceptualization of culture as static and essential has attracted criticism. Some culture experts claim to have found inconsistencies in both its theory and methodology.[64] Many think that he identifies cultures with nations based on the supposition that within each nation there is a uniform national culture, a suggestion Hofstede explicitly denies when he insists on the resilience to change in spite of all this diversity.

Conclusion

Values are critical determinants of our behavior; they represent our highest priorities and our most deep-seated driving forces. Values are priorities that tell us how to allocate our limited resources (e.g., our time and energy), right here, right now. And these priorities matter. It is critical to our satisfaction, health, fulfillment, happiness that we understand them and their consequences. This is why:

---

[64]   See, for example: Taras, V., Kirkman, B. L., & Steel, P. (2010). Examining the impact of *Culture's Consequences*: A three-decade, multilevel, meta-analytic review of Hofstede's cultural value dimensions. *Journal of Applied Psychology*, *95*(3), 405–439.

1. Time is our most limited resource; time does not renew itself. Once we spend a day, it's gone forever. If we waste that day by investing our time in actions that don't produce the results we want, that loss is permanent. We can earn more money, improve our physical bodies, and repair broken relationships, but we can not redo yesterday. If we had infinite time, then values and priorities would be irrelevant. But our life spans are limited, and if we value our mortal lives, then it makes sense that we'd want to invest them as best we can.

2. Human beings tend to be fairly inconsistent in how we invest our time and energy. Most of us are easily distracted. It's easy to fall into the trap of living by different priorities every day. One day we exercise; the next day we slack off. One day we work productively; the next day we are stricken with a bout of laziness. If we don't consciously use our priorities to stick to a clear and consistent course, we will naturally drift off course and shift all over the place. And this kind of living yields poor results. Imagine an airplane that went wherever the wind took it: Who knows where it would eventually land? And the flight itself would likely be stressful and uncertain.

Our limited time and typically low index of distraction make it extremely important that we know what our values are and consciously live by them.

Our values are informed by everything that has happened in our lives and everyone we've known—our parents and family, our religious affiliation, our friends and peers, our education, our reading, and more. Effective people recognize these environmental influences and identify and develop a clear, concise, and meaningful set of beliefs, values, and priorities. They also recognize that some values may be more important than others in a given moment or context. Our personal hierarchy of values must be versatile; it needs to be refined, tuned, and synchronized with our surroundings (family, friends, workplace, community).

When we join an organization, community, or family, we bring our deeply held values and beliefs with us. There they co-mingle with those of the other members to create an organization or family or community culture. But the subject is a little more complicated than this. As we've seen, existing organizations already have a deeply embedded set of values, as do nations, communities, and families. These determine their behaviors and may or may not agree with their espoused values, which are much easier to identify. In addition, the structures of these systems often give some people more power than others to establish or shift entrenched values. What do we do if we begin to feel uncomfortable in our surroundings or start to sense a disconnect from the cultures in which we live and work?

Sometimes we need help understanding our values. We also may need help understanding the culture and values of the places in which we live and work—especially in today's increasingly culturally diverse environments. Coaches can play a major role in helping people understand their values and the values of their surroundings. Coaches can also help people make choices and adapt, creating a positive fit between people and their surroundings. Sometimes the choice may be to find a situation more in sync with your values. Or it may mean working hard on yourself or in concert with your partner, team, or organization. Whatever we need to do to attain it, a positive fit makes for a happier person, and a happier person will be more successful. We will learn more about how to create this fit in the remaining chapters.

CBV Reflection ♣ ♠ ♥

Think of the key message(s) that you retained after reading this chapter. Then complete the following sentences:

The principal point(s) I liked in this chapter include

1._____
2._____
3._____

The principal point(s) that I did not like or disagreed with in this chapter include

1._____
2._____
3._____

Complete this section only if you are already a professional coach:

After reading this chapter, I am intrigued by the 3Es tri-axial model of values because I can see its potential utility for

1._____
2._____
3._____

Chapter 3

The Secret of Coaching by Values:
Alignment and Realignment

- 3.1 If the shoe fits, wear it; if it doesn't, change it

- 3.2 The importance of reshaping and realigning values

- 3.3 Value congruence and positive outcomes

- 3.4 The negative consequences of value incongruence

- Conclusion

3.1 If the shoe fits, wear it; if it doesn't, change it

I will start with a metaphor. Try and walk for a while in shoes that don't fit. What will happen? If the shoes are too small, you will start to feel the pain after a few steps. The pain will grow gradually to the point that you can not take it any longer, and you will change the shoes. The same thing will happen (though it will take a little longer) if you walk in shoes that are too big. First, you will slide a bit inside; your socks will tear, but there won't be any physical damage. But if you keep walking, for longer distances and repeatedly, you will feel the impact of the oversize shoes. Now, what would you think if people said to you, "You really need to adjust your feet to fit the shoes." Wouldn't it be more reasonable to just adjust—or change—the shoes? And if you can't find the proper shoes in Store 1, you will shop around until you find them. This could take a while, and the new shoes may not fit forever, but they will provide the comfort you need at the time—and your life will be better for it.

The same thing happens with values. If your values (whatever they are) do not fit the values of your spouse, your team, your organization, your community, or even your country, you will feel miserable; you will sense a misfit, and the growing psychological pain will end up in physical pain. It is normal for people to look for the right culture, one in which they feel a better (if not perfect) fit between their values and the values of their environment.

Do organizations offer us new shoes, or do they expect us to readjust to the shoes offered? Almost always, they expect us to adjust. The reasons organizations developed, and in some cases continue to maintain, cultures characterized by rules, regulations, and control is that they are easier to manage, they worked well for centuries, and they derive from the paradigm of efficiency (producing more with fewer resources). Organizations today have to struggle with the tension of exercising control on one hand and developing their employees on the other.

A great majority of companies today are strategically designed according to traditional organizational models oriented toward hierarchical control. An over-reliance on control and rational processes, while relatively comfortable and predictable, contributes to an environment in which employees are indifferent, uninspired, and excessively dependent on leadership. I am not suggesting that control is bad, but I strongly believe that a more integrated,[65] flexible, and learning-oriented design will contribute to a robust culture and therefore a successful business.

Resolving the dilemma between security and risk (between control and development) is essential to the survival and growth of an organization. Both options imply certain distinct, but related, systems of values. My consulting experience has taught me that a company that clings to values of concentration, preferring rigid departmental boundaries and a parochial view to an open-minded and forward-thinking vision, is very likely to stagnate, because it will not be receptive to changes in the environment (e.g., market demands, new technologies, resources). Excessive order and control causes loss of vitality and drive. Companies have been known to die of boredom, not just figuratively but literally; their best people have gotten fed up and left. Take the "Control vs. Development Values Quiz" in this chapter to see where your organization (or family or team; see NOTE below the quiz) lies along the control-development values continuum. The second part of the quiz will let you begin to see how well your values are aligned with those of your organization.

---

[65] By a more integrated design, I mean one in which relevant aspects of control and development are woven throughout the organization.

CBV Reflection ♣ ♠ ♥

Control vs. Development Values Quiz

(*NOTE: This quiz was created for organizational settings, but it works for families and small groups; just slightly adjust the questions)

A. Rate the following elements of your organization* from 0 through 5 according to the given characteristics:

		0	1	2	3	4	5
1.	Structure	fluid					rigid
2.	Innovation	high					low
3.	Risk orientation	risk taking					risk averting
4.	Vision	wide/global					narrow/local
5.	General orientation	process					results
6.	Conformity	low pressure					high pressure
7.	Learning climate	relearning					retention
8.	Changes	embraced					resisted
9.	Tolerance to diversity	high					low
10.	Task orientation	multitasking					specialized tasking

.

Add your answers to get your organization's total score: [   ]

Interpret your score:
0–15   Your organization seem to be development-oriented
35–50   Your organization seem to be control-oriented

B. Assess your own values and preferences. Think about your values and general preferences, and think about the kind of organization in which you like to work. Fill out the quick-scoring quiz below. On the right-hand side, put any number from 0 through 5.

I prefer to work in (or be associated with) a culture where there is

1. Fluid structure (0) .... Rigid structure (5)   ____

2. High innovation (0).................Low innovation (5)   ____

3. Risk taking (0) ....Risk averting (5)   ____

4. Wide/global vision (0)..............Narrow/local vision (5)   ____

5. Process orientation (0).............Results orientation (5)   ____

6. Low pressure to conform (0)...... High pressure to conform (5)   ____

7. Learning climate (0)...............Retention climate (5)   ____

8. Openness to change (0)...........Resistance to change (5)   ____

9. High diversity tolerance (0)......Low diversity tolerance (5)   ____

10. Multitasking orientation (0)....Specialized task orientation (5)   ____

Total score [   ]

Interpret your score:
0–15 You seem to have preference for development-oriented cultures
35–50 You seem to have preference for control-oriented cultures

Now, calculate the gap between the two scores. It is the size of the gap that causes discomfort. Remember the metaphor of the shoe. Oversize shoes and undersize shoes can cause similar discomfort. The smaller the gap, the more the congruence (or fit) and the less difficult it will be to be involved in a change process. The larger the gap, the more challenging achieving congruence will be from a coaching perspective.

The meaning of values: Control-oriented organizations vs. learning, or development-oriented, organizations

Values, as we saw in the last chapter, are concepts that we identify and define using words. We name our values. But the names (the words) we give them may be used in very different ways to mean very different things according to the context. Most cultures (organizations, nations, families, and others) think of "good" as a value to be prized. But for some, being good means being resigned and patient, whereas for others, it means being enterprising and original, having the courage to say what one thinks or believes. The word is the same, but it represents two very different ways of being. Similarly, values such as support, respect, integrity, and efficiency can take on a variety of meanings depending on whether they are formulated in a culture oriented toward control or in a culture focused on learning and development. In this and the next few sections, I will focus on the meaning of values in organizations, but the thinking can be applied to values in any culture, system, or environment.

A culture of learning and development is rooted in values that support and encourage both organizational and human potential. Often these distinctions are thought of as twentieth-century versus twenty-first-century organizational cultures or simply, old versus new, or traditional versus innovative, cultures. Exhibit 3.1 compares the entirely different meanings certain values have in both cultural types.

Exhibit 3.1 Meanings of specific values: Culture of control and culture of development

Values	20th century: culture of control	21st century: culture of learning and development
Control	Supervision focused on control geared toward correcting deviations from anticipated results. Results are determined by top management. Hierarchical structure.	Managers encourage autonomy and employee responsibility. Control is interwoven in policies and procedures to ensure quality assurance, safety, etc. Results are derived through participatory processes that are inclusive and aimed at getting appropriate and accurate information. Flatter organizational structure.
Support	Saying what you believe others want to hear; approving and praising; helping to hide errors.	Helping others to check the effectiveness of their work and learning from their errors.
Integrity	Staying put in one's own principles, values and beliefs; not giving in.	Open disposition toward situations and others with different belief systems.
Respect	Not questioning the rationale of other people and more specifically those in positions of authority.	Show consideration for others regardless of organizational 'rank' and being open to their opinion, ideas, perspective, etc.
Self-confidence	Demonstrating self-confidence through persuasion and 'winning.' Admission of errors is akin to 'losing face' and status. Posturing is a way of life.	Demonstrating self-confidence as well as accepting other opinions. Capacity to admit mistakes, learn from others regardless of position.

3.2 The importance of reshaping and realigning values

Organizational leaders spend too much time drafting and redrafting vision statements, mission statements, values statements, purpose statements, aspiration statements, and so on. They spend nowhere near enough time trying to understand the nature of alignment of their organizations with the values and visions already in place.

Researching, and sometimes working closely with, some of the world's most visionary organizations has made it clear to me that they concentrate primarily on the process of alignment rather than on diagnosing and understanding what kind of alignment is really needed. To do that, we need to again and again come back to the basics and ask fundamental questions like, What are our core values? What is our primary reason for existing? What do we aspire to achieve and become? These are very important questions that get at the true vision of an organization.[66]

Vision is one of the least understood, and most overused, words. Vision is simply a combination of three basic elements of an organization: (1) its fundamental reason for existing beyond just making money (often called its "mission" or "purpose"), (2) its timeless unchanging core values, and (3) huge and audacious—but ultimately achievable—aspirations for its future. Of these, the most important element of great, enduring organizations are its core values.

There is a big difference between being an organization with a vision statement and a truly visionary organization. The difference lies in creating alignment—alignment to preserve an organization's core values, to reinforce its purpose, and to stimulate continued progress toward its aspirations. When you have superb alignment, a visitor could drop into your organization from another planet and infer the vision without having to read it on paper.

Creating alignment is a two-part process. The first is identifying and correcting misalignments. The second is creating new alignments, or what I call "reengineering the culture with mechanisms of real reinforcement."

---

[66] For a more thorough discussion of vision and mission, see: Dolan, S. L., Garcia, S., & Richley, B. (2006). *Managing by Values: Corporate Guide to Living, Being Alive and Making a Living in the 21ˢᵗ Century*. London: Palgrave Macmillan.

Correcting misalignments

Identifying misalignments means looking around the organization, talking to people, getting input, conducting organization culture audits, and asking, If these are our core values and this is fundamentally why we exist, what are the obstacles that get in our way? For instance, many organizations say they respect and trust their people to do the right thing, but they undermine that statement by doing X, Y, and Z. The misalignments exist not because the statements are false; these companies believe what they say. The misalignments occur because years of ad hoc policies and practices have become institutionalized and have obscured the firm's underlying values. The first task for leaders, then, is to create an environment and a process that enable people to safely identify and eliminate these misalignments.

The task of a business coach is to show senior executives the misalignments, to discuss the consequences, and to help the leader develop a policy for encouraging open debate and dialogue around the core values.

Exhibit 3.2A Corporate alignment strategy

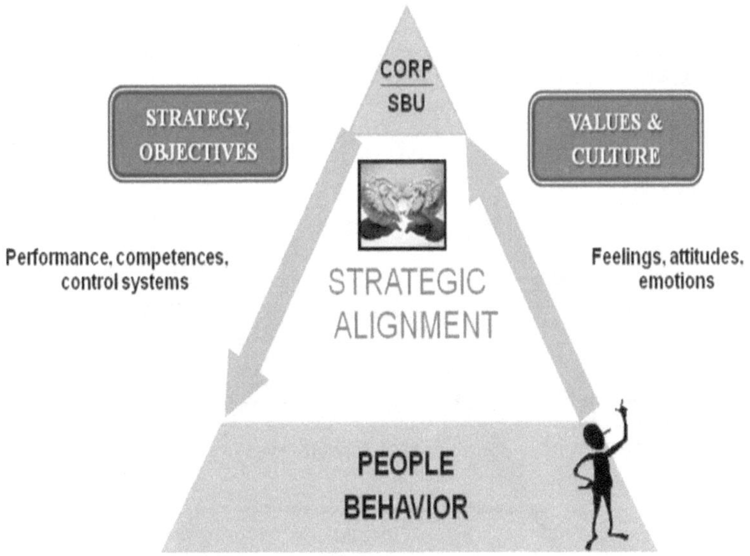

CORP
SBU

STRATEGY, OBJECTIVES

VALUES & CULTURE

Performance, competences, control systems

Feelings, attitudes, emotions

STRATEGIC ALIGNMENT

PEOPLE BEHAVIOR

Exhibit 3.2A presents an example of a corporate alignment strategy. Note that both arrows in the graphic are complete; there are no breaks in them. Information is flowing throughout all levels of the organization. There is a balance between the left and right sides of the triangle. How often is such a strategy really followed? In most cases, when senior members of an organization craft strategies to align people's behavior with the corporation's goals, they do not recognize that complete alignment requires both sides of the triangle—the left side (strategy and control) and the right side (values and culture)—and input from all members.

Most companies rely on a unit called SBU (Strategic Business Unit) to develop their goals and objectives and to formulate strategies to align people's behavior with these goals. For years, companies tried to force alignment by focusing on the left side of the figure in exhibit 3.2A: crafting performance standards, ensuring technical competences, and employing a variety of control systems (e.g., titles, perks, salaries, promotions, withholding promotions). This is like using only the left hemisphere of the brain (rational thinking and linear reasoning). And for a long time it worked; it produced good results. However, today's workforce is by far more educated and less susceptible to manipulation. At the same time, the environment is far more complex (nonlinear) and becoming even more so. In this kind of business environment, organizations that fail to also use the right side of the brain (more artistic, more poetic, more sensitive) and listen to the people in the organization will not be able to create an alignment.

Exhibit 3.2B: Why so many companies fail to achieve strategic alignment

In exhibit 3.2B, we see why corporate "alignment" strategies so often fail. They are in fact "misalignment" strategies and look more like exhibit 3.2B than 3.2A. When people's feelings, attitudes, and emotions are not aligned with the organization, the brain will not be aligned, and the entire system will not work. To create a better alignment, we need to work simultaneously with the two sides of the brain.

There are ample books, writings, and consulting firms claiming they can help any organization enhance performance by setting objectives, developing incentives and control measures, crafting policies, and initiating practices connected with the rational paradigm (left side). But the right side has not been given nearly as much attention. To help remedy this, let us look at the values and culture side of the equation.

Creating new alignments

Creating something that doesn't yet exist but ought to is not easy. True alignment means being creatively compulsive. It means going over the top. It requires a combination of factors and conditions. The most important are openness and the will to change. Overcoming resistance to change and sponsoring a process of culture reengineering requires a courageous leader. One who is not afraid to take a risk. One who understands that it is not possible to *set* organizational values; it is only possible to *discover* them. Nor can you "install" new core values into people. Core values are not something people buy in to; they must be predisposed to holding them. Thus, the task for the leader is either a) finding people who are already predisposed to sharing her core values or b) changing and adapting to the core values of the rest of the members of the organization.

The process of culture reengineering involves identifying the core values, identifying gaps between the core values and the mission and vision, attracting and retaining people who share the core values, and letting people who aren't predisposed to sharing these values go elsewhere. This last action may sound harsh, but you can do this by showing people that this might be good for *them*, because it opens up opportunities for them to find situations in which they will be happier and more likely to succeed. Leaving an organization, a country, a community, or a family is not necessarily a bad thing.

Every institution, team, group, family, or enterprise has to wrestle with this vexing question: What should change and what should never change? It's a matter of distinguishing timeless core values from operating practices and cultural norms. Timeless core values should never change; operating practices and cultural norms should never stop changing. Timeless core values in a family are respect for each other and trust in each other. This should never change. At a university, a core value should be freedom of intellectual inquiry. The moment this core value begins to wither, the institution risks losing the vision necessary for it to advance and create new knowledge. But going back to the critical question above, it's important not to conflate core values with other things. At times, institutions cling doggedly to practices that are in truth nothing more than familiar habits. As a result, they fail to change things that ought to change. And by defending outmoded practices under the banner of core values, they might actually be betraying their true core values.

Many organizations exist with value misalignment. Many leaders forget about the importance of values. Few institutions take responsibility for value alignment. An inflexible hierarchy, overdependence on competition, and constraints on behavior guarantee frustration in any environment. Value alignment is critical to successful organizational endeavors. In the next sections, I will provide a quick overview of the research showing the concrete positive consequences of value alignment (value congruence) and the negative consequences of value misalignment (value incongruence).

Before moving to the next section, take a moment to list the possible consequences of congruence and incongruence in any environment in which you work or live by doing the Consequences of Value Incongruence and Value Congruence exercise.

CBV Reflection ♣ ♠ ♥

Consequences of Value Incongruence and Value Congruence

Jot down of the possible key consequences of incongruence (left column) and congruence (right column) between your values and the values of your environment (e.g., your company, your team, your family or partner, your workgroup).

If you are discussing this in a team, see if the team can identify the 10 most important consequences of value incongruence (anything positive or negative such as performance, motivation, and health, just to mention a few), and the 10 most obvious possible consequences of value congruence.

Possible significant consequences of value incongruence	Possible significant consequences of perfect (or near perfect) value congruence

The Value of Values in the Coaching Experience

Dave Ulrich

A few years ago, I was honored to be invited to coach a high potential leader in a large company. He had the many of the technical skills that predicted his success, but the executives felt that his softer skills could use improvement. So he agreed to coaching. When I asked him why he was interested in being coached, he said because he was told it would be good for him. When I asked why I was considered as his possible coach, he said because I was known in some coaching circles and he could tell others he was being coached by me. It was my shortest coaching experience ever. When I left after cutting short my interview, I told the HR leader that this high potential individual was not prepared to coach or to learn. He saw coaching not as a commitment to change but as another "check" on his rise to executive ranks and his name-dropping of his coach as a point of personal pride.

I have often reflected on this experience. What did I learn? I realized the "value of values" in coaching and being coached.

Value focuses outside; values come from within. Value emphasizes what others get from our efforts; values emphasize who we are. Value can be created and developed through innovation and hard work; values are generally inherited and may be honed through self-awareness and experience. Value can be measured by impact; values are measured by the strength of our character. Value derives from the worth of our work to stakeholders; values reflect the worth of our work to us.

As a coach, my value is created when I help those I coach understand their values and learn how to use their values to create value for others. When my values as a coach do not align with the values of those I coach, the experience will fail for both of us.

As a coachee, the value of coaching comes not only from learning about oneself but also from learning how one's personal values (and style, behaviors, and predispositions) do or do not create value for others. Being coached requires being willing to look into a values mirror to determine how one can make personal changes that help others.

To understand the value of values, we believe we have to start with the "why" question. Psychologist Wendy Ulrich and I spent the last few years trying to figure out why people work and how their reasons for work both reflect their values and affect the value they create for others. We discovered that people find more value in, derive more value from, and add more value to their work when they know why they do it.

In the book *The Why of Work*, we identify seven factors—and corresponding questions—leaders leaders can explore to become meaning-makers who help employees recognize the values that drive them at work and thus deliver more value from the work they do. Exploring these factors and asking these questions (slightly revised for coaches), can provide coaches and coachees personal insights about how their personal values can help them deliver more value through coaching:

1. **Identity:** What do I want to be known for as a coach? How does my approach to coaching reflect my strengths so that they will strengthen others? How can I help my clients (coachees) better recognize their strengths and use them to serve others?

2. **Purpose:** What do I want to accomplish as a coach? What do I want my clients to leave my coaching experience more able to know and/or do? How do I help my clients recognize and clarify their personal aspirations and definitions of success?

3. **Relationships:** How can I form personal relationships with those I coach in a professional setting? How can I overlook the foibles of those I coach and care for them? How can I help those I coach learn to surround themselves with personal relationships that are supportive?

4. **Work environment:** How do I coach individuals so that they can understand and adapt to the work environment in which they work? How can I build a positive work environment in the microcosm of the coaching experience? How can I help my clients be sensitive to the work environment they create by their actions and decisions?

5. **Work itself:** What is it about coaching that is energizing and exciting to me as a coach? What do I like about the work that I

do? How do I help my clients discover the work that energizes them?

6. **Learning and growth:** What am I learning as a coach? How am I different because of each coaching experience? How can I help my clients desire and recognize their learning agility?

7. **Fun:** How can I have fun even in the midst of demanding coaching assignments? How can I help my clients recognize the playful side of their lives even as they accept increased responsibilities and accountabilities?

In *Why of Work*, we argue that leaders who resolve these seven domains become meaning-makers who build abundant organizations that make cents (money) and sense (purpose). I suggest that coaches and coachees who reflect on these questions will discover that coaching is a way to create the value of values.

Had the individual I met and did not coach worked through these questions, or had I been more explicit about them, both he and I would have had a better experience.

Dave Ulrich is a professor of business administration at Ross School of Business, University of Michigan, and cofounder of the RBL Group. He serves on the board of directors of Herman Miller and the board of trustees of Southern Virginia University and is a Fellow of the National Academy of Human Resources. He has written 23 books that cover topics in HR, leadership, and organizations. For more on Ulrich, his work, and his publications, go to www.daveulrich.com.

3.3 Value alignment and positive outcomes

Value alignment and positive organizational outcomes

The term *value alignment*, or as it often called in in the coaching field, *value congruence* or *value fit*, has received much attention lately from both scientists and business leaders. The concept of value congruence is intuitive; when there is a match between the employee's and the organization's value systems, positive outcomes will result. In this section, I will explain the benefits of value congruence—and the negative consequences of values incongruence—as I see them.

In previous chapters, we saw that both individuals and organizations have value systems that dictate their attitudes and behaviors and the ways in which they allocate resources. Research has shown that value congruence can lead to several valuable outcomes for both the organization and the individual:[67]

- **Job satisfaction:** Job satisfaction is a positive emotional experience associated with one's job. Satisfied employees are more productive and experience less stress than dissatisfied employees.

- **Organizational identification and commitment:** Organizational identification derives from an employee's sense of belonging to the organization. Employees who feel like they belong are likely to be more committed to the organization, more productive, and more likely to engage in extra-role behaviors, helping behaviors that go beyond the duties of one's position.

- **Intent to stay:** Intent to stay is an employee's intent to remain with the organization over some period of time. Intent to stay is contingent on job satisfaction and organizational identification.

---

[67] This summary is based on two excellent pieces of recent research: Edwards, J. R., & Cable, D. M. (2009). The value of value congruence. *Journal of Applied Psychology, 94*(3), 654–677; Bao, Y., Dolan, S. L., & Grau, M. (2010, June). *Exploring the construct of value congruence and its proposed effect on work engagement and organizational citizenship behavior: A positive organizational behavior perspective.* Paper presented at the 12th biennial conference of the International Society for the Study of Work and Organizational Behavior (ISSWOV), Estoril, Portugal.

- **Performance:** When a person has the knowledge and skills to perform well, value congruence can lead to even better performance by positively affecting job satisfaction, organizational identification, and commitment.

- **Reduced conflicts:** Value congruence decreases conflicts. Group value consensus has been found to be a key factor in reducing conflicts.

Although the link between value congruence and positive organizational outcomes has been firmly established, until recently it was not clear how value congruence leads to such outcomes. Some research indicates that value congruence directly effects positive organizational outcomes, and other research proposes that value congruence results in positive outcomes indirectly by enhancing communication and trust between the organization and the employee. Exhibit 3.3 shows the proposed sequence from value congruence to positive outcomes.

Exhibit 3.3: Proposed chain from value congruence to positive outcomes

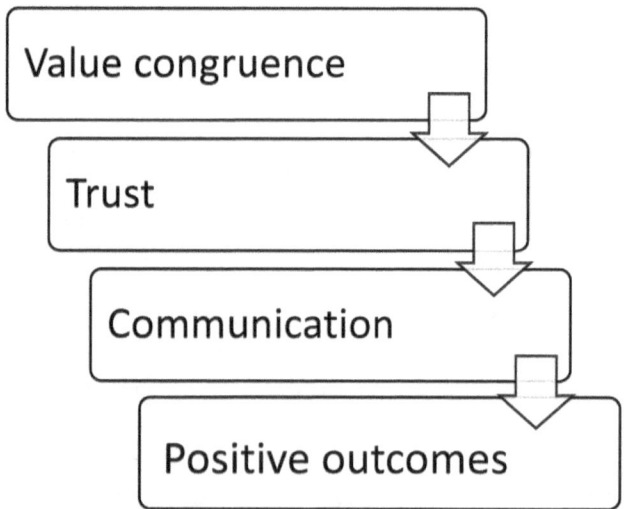

Recently new positive outcomes of value congruence have surfaced in the work and organizational behavior literature: OCB (Organizational Citizenship Behavior) and enhanced work engagement. The early evidence suggests that when value congruence occurs between an employee and his or her organization, organizational citizenship behaviors (OCBs) results. These are behaviors that go beyond an employee's written job description and are not a part of his or her formal job requirements. They contribute to overall organizational functioning. The ability of managers to direct the values of employees toward organizational goals greatly affects the degree to which the employees engage in OCBs throughout their careers.

Work engagement is a positive, fulfilling, work-related state of mind that is characterized by vigor, dedication, and absorption. The findings of work engagement scholars suggest that engaged workers have high energy, high self-efficacy, and a positive attitude about work and life. Despite the lack of systematic research connecting the two, my experience has shown a strong link between value congruence and work engagement. In its high form, it can become what positive psychologists call "flow." Flow is the mental state of operation in which a person in an activity is fully immersed in a feeling of energized focus and complete involvement in the process of the activity and is able to achieve goals and objectives successfully. Flow is completely focused motivation. It is single-minded immersion and represents perhaps the ultimate in harnessing emotions in the service of performing and learning. When one is in flow, his or her emotions are not just contained and channeled, but positive, energized, and aligned with the task at hand. The hallmark of flow is a feeling of spontaneous joy, even rapture, while performing a task.[68]

In sum, individuals are more comfortable in organizations that are consistent with their own values. The congruence of personal and organizational values enables employees to feel a connection to the company and its mission. To gain a competitive advantage within the industry, organizations need employees who will go well beyond their expected work responsibilities. Aligning values and enhancing congruence seem to lead to multiple direct and indirect positive outcomes.

Does value congruence enhance mental and physical health?

With the emergence of positive psychology,[69] we are learning more and more about the positive aspects of health and well-being. Value

---

[68] To read more about the concept of flow, see: Csikszentmihalyi, M. (1988). The flow experience and its significance for human psychology. In *Optimal experience: psychological studies of flow in consciousness* (pp. 15–35). Cambridge, UK: Cambridge University Press.

[69] Positive psychology defines itself as a "science of positive subjective experience, positive individual traits, and positive institutions" that seeks to "understand

congruence leads to work engagement, which has been found to enhance mental health as well as psychosomatic health. Value congruence also leads to relative happiness, which in turn has been correlated with both mental and physical health.

Positive psychology focuses on positive emotions, strengths, and good mental health, all of which are related to value congruence. Happiness and life satisfaction are linked to value congruence. My colleagues and I have seen that value congruence coupled with support and optimism leads to faster recovery following surgery. Although some people take it even further and suggest that there is a link between positive psychology and cancer survival, this has yet to be proven.

While wellness is experienced at the individual level as happiness, joy, health, and longevity, many of its causal factors extend well beyond the individual. Similarly, while wellness promotion strives to increase the joy, health, and longevity of individuals, its strategies go well beyond the individual and include environmental, social, and other collective interventions because the etiology of wellness and well-being depends on, among other factors, value congruence (the social environment) and the physical environment.

The research stemming from positive psychology on subjective well-being, positive affect, and life satisfaction; the development of the Values in Action Classification of Strengths; and the study of how those strengths can be applied by individuals to improve their social interactions are all very important additions to the evolving explanation of the enhancement of well-being.[70]

3.4 The negative consequences of value incongruence

One thing is certain, a prolonged state of value incongruence leads to stress, and stress is a condition that debilitates the body and the soul. I have written many articles and books on the sources and consequences

---

and build the factors that allow individuals, communities, and societies to flourish."

[70] Seligman, M. E. P., & Csikszentmihalyi, M. (2000). Positive psychology: An introduction. *American Psychologist, 55*, 5–14.

of stress (at work), and as I mentioned in the last chapter, I am convinced that the latter negatively affects our physical and mental health.[71]

There has been ample research on stress in the past 30 years or so, even if—as I suggested in the last chapter—the knowledge it has generated has not permeated our lives and work. Interestingly, though, the medical and biological literature has started to borrow concepts from psychology and sociology, such as stress, to explain mutation of cells (or diseases). Traditional medical textbooks classify diseases by the organ system affected and frequently by the agent involved, for example, viral, rickettsial, and bacterial diseases. But increasingly, mental and physical diseases are appearing that cannot be explained sufficiently in this manner—among them some illnesses that we now know are related to stress. The models of diseases have changed and the new paradigms include social phenomenon in the etiology of a disease. One of the social factors that has been identified in this context is value incongruence (see, for example, exhibit 3.4, which shows a proposed etiological chain of disease published in a 1974 medical journal).

When an individual experiences chronic value incongruence, the likelihood of health-related problems increases dramatically. In our own research, my colleagues and I found out that nurses who felt trapped in their jobs (they wanted out because of value incongruence) but were forced to stay in their positions by economic needs, experience a higher level of job burnout, and also have a higher incidence of metabolic syndrome than expected given their age.[72] Metabolic syndrome is considered a key predictor for heart disease and type 2 diabetes. Burnout—an unpleasant and dysfunctional condition that both individuals and organizations would like to avoid—has been established to be a stress phenomenon. It presents the pattern of health correlates one expects to find in such a condition: headaches, gastrointestinal disorders, muscle tension,

---

[71] Dolan, S. L. (2006). *Stress, Self-Esteem, Health and Work*. London. Palgrave Macmillan; Dolan, S. L., Arsenault, A. (2009). *Stress, Estime de soi, Santé et Travail*. Montréal: Presse de l'Université du Québec.

[72] Moodie, S., Dolan, S. L., & Arsenault, A. (2011, February 24–27). *Exploring the multiple linkages between metabolic syndrome and stress: An empirical analysis of the relationships between stress, health, and metabolic syndrome among Catalan nurses*. Paper presented at International Conference on Prehypertension & Cardio-Metabolic Syndrome, Vienna, Austria.

hypertension, cold/flu episodes, and sleep disturbances, among others. It is also a form of mental distress characterized by a) a predominance of dysphoric symptoms such as emotional exhaustion, b) a predominance of mental and behavioral symptoms, and c) decreased work performance resulting from negative attitudes and behaviors.

Exhibit 3.4: The etiological chain

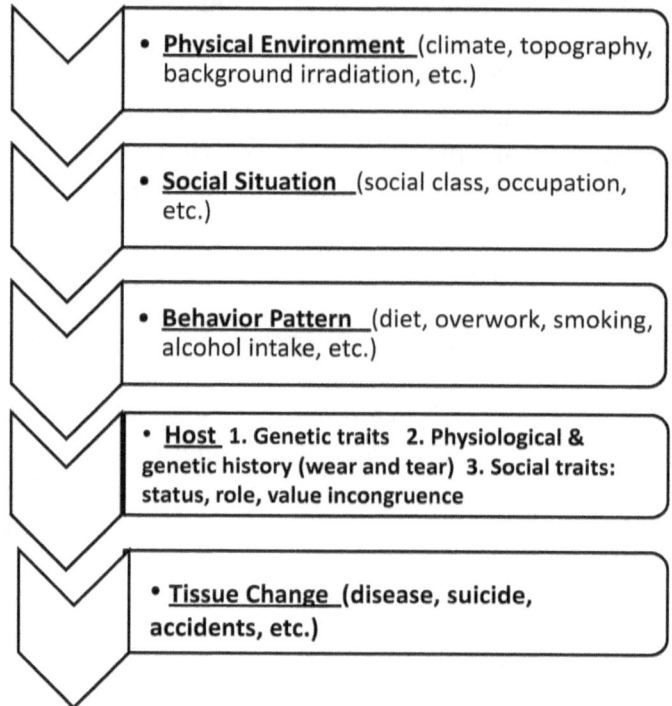

SOURCE: Modified from Saxon, G. (1974, November). The sociological approach to epidemiology. *American Journal of Public Health (AJPH)*, *64*(11), 1046–1049.

The scientific evidence for negative outcomes of chronic value incongruence for both organizations (e.g., productivity loss, incapacity to retain talent) and individuals (e.g., likelihood of mental and physical diseases) is overwhelming. I am not talking about a form of temporary or transitory incongruence; I am talking about a permanent feeling or a permanent perception. Just think about yourself. What do you think will happen to you if you feel completely and continually incongruent with your partner? With your family and friends? With your organization or your community? The likelihood that it will affect your mental and physical health is very high.

Despite the obvious connections, the relationships between values, cognitions, stress, and illnesses are complex and not fully understood. But science is advancing our understanding of psychological experiences. We now know that these experiences in some ways both arise from (or are manifestations of) and affect brain chemistry and biology. It appears that cognitions leading to stress have an effect on biology. A basic example of this is that when we are stressed, we experience muscle tension and increased heart rate. The strength of the relationship between thoughts and pathologies such as cancer cannot yet be determined, and because of this, I'd view any absolute statements about this with a healthy skepticism. Nonetheless, coaching advice and interventions to improve psychological health by reducing incongruence among values will likely be beneficial not only for enhancing mental health and quality of life, but also potentially for increasing physical health. This is not to suggest that coaches are therapists, but it is important to recognize that reducing incongruence will have multiple positive effects on overall health.

Several theories from different research fields in management, psychology, and medicine claim that human beings are generally inclined to reduce cognitive or motivational discrepancies, and that such incongruences are associated with negative outcomes, such as psychological distress or dissatisfaction. So, by and large, high levels of incongruence are hypothesized to be an essential cause of the formation and maintenance of a variety of psychopathological symptoms.

CBV Reflection ♣ ♠ ♥

Discovering Congruence: Write Your Obituary

Here is an interesting way to self-diagnose congruence and incongruence in your life. To do this, you need to be a) totally honest and b) creative.

As a celebration of life, help write your obituary. Think of what others in your life will say

1. about the differences between what you say and what you do

2. which key values they would have liked you to exhibit to be congruent with their expectation?

What would your life partner say about you?	
What would your children say about you?	
What would your friends say about you?	
What would your co-workers (or business partners) say about you?	
What would your parents say about you?	
What would your neighbors say about you?	

When you have completed it, post this form on your refrigerator for members of your family and e-mail it to friends, neighbors, and colleagues. Let each of them respond and correct. Then ask yourself, "Do I need to make any adjustments?" After reflection and discussion with your coach (or friends and family), make a shorter list of adjustments you need to make.

My coherent behavior and legacy:

> I want to be remembered for

Discuss this short legacy with your coach (or family and friends) and use the analysis to plan future changes in your behavior; it is another exercise in value alignment.

Conclusion

The name of the game is value realignment. Throughout this chapter, I have tried to show why we need to pause, assess our values, compare them with those of our cultures or environments (partner, family, colleagues, organization, or the entire community), and see if there are discrepancies, or incongruences, that require realignment. I showed that poor alignment will likely negatively affect our health and the people around us. Also, our productivity will suffer. Alternatively, while it is not certain that enhancing congruence will lead directly to enhanced well-being, the likelihood that it will is high, and certainly it will enhance wellness and general happiness. There is strong evidence that in work contexts, congruence between a person's values and those of his or her job, work, or organization leads to more meaningful work, higher levels of engagement, and improved performance.

In the next chapter, I will show how you can put value congruence to work in your organization, in your family, or even in your community using techniques for value realignment. Value realignment is not entirely a new concept. But the methodology I present in this book, based on the 3Es tri-axial model, is unique. I will describe this methodology in detail in the next chapter.

CBV Reflection ♣ ♠ ♥

Think of the key message(s) you retained after reading this chapter. Then complete the following sentences:

The principal points I liked in this chapter include

1._____
2._____
3._____

The principal points that I did not like or disagreed with in this chapter include

1._____
2._____
3._____

Chapter 4

CBV Methodologies and Tools for Everyone

- 4.1 Values and success in the life of business and the business of life

- 4.2 CBV methods for reengineering the business of life

- 4.3 The Gift of Values: A coaching enrichment module

- 4.4 CBV processes, methods, tools for reengineering the life of business

- Conclusion

4.1 Values and success in the life of business and the business of life

Throughout this book, I have emphasized that values act as our compass. This compass keeps us on course every single day and brings us back if we've drifted away. If we follow our compass, each day we will move in a direction that takes us closer to what we envision as the "best" life possible. This best, of course, is very individual. Your best may not be—and likely isn't—my best. And even though neither of us may ever reach our ideal, as we proceed along the path toward it, we will enjoy increasingly positive states of well-being.

Much of life exists on a continuum. There are some discrete markers like marriage or having children: One is either married or not married (though even this may have shades of gray, and marriage means different things to different people and in different cultures); one either has children or doesn't. But most things are achieved gradually: Health, financial status, relationship intimacy, and happiness come in degrees; they are changeable; they get better and worse. Rarely can anyone instantly achieve the state of "best" in any of these areas. But one hopes that cumulatively, the "betters" increase throughout one's life. I think it is safe to say that for most of us, more health, happiness, wealth, intimacy, inner peace, and love is better than less.

Moreover, because everyone has a different definition of the best life, some things mean more to one person than to another. For some people, good health is an absolute must. For others, being compassionate is what's most important. And for each of these values, every person is at a different point along his or her own continuum. Let us go back to metaphor of the airplane in chapter 2. Imagine that there are now several airplanes in the air, each having taken off from a different location and heading for a different destination airport, a different best. It's impossible to plot one course that would bring every plane to its desired airport. Each plane requires its own individual course.

Continuing this conceit, let's say that the planes and their routes represent not different people, but the trajectory of different values in one individual's life. Each person is in a different state of health right now, and each person is aiming for a different best possible health. So the course each person takes from his or her unique starting point to her own best state of health will be different. Because we cannot do everything at once and we have limited time, we have to prioritize. We may not be able to land all the planes within the span of our lives because we most likely do not know how long our lives will be; nor can we be certain how long it will take us to land each of these planes. But the closer we bring each plane to its destination airport, the better that area of life will be.

The journey to your values: A generic methodology, a dyad method, and corporate action plans

In this chapter, I hope to give you a deep understanding of the processes of alignment and realignment, or reengineering. I will set the stage by laying out an overall methodology, which can be transferred to various settings, cultures, and environments by adjusting the procedures involved. This step-by-step process will show you how to create a personal values hierarchy and align it with your goals. You can use it to get a sense of whether your life in general is going in the direction you want it, and you can use it to analyze specific areas of life (e.g., work, marriage, friendships, and other relationships); with this basic method, you will be able to create a values hierarchy for any context or culture and determine whether it is congruent with yours. This is the generic Coaching by Values (CBV) method.[73]

You can work through the CBV process with or without a coach; I will point out steps at which a coach's intervention may be helpful. If you are working through it yourself, and at the end you have not achieved congruence, you may want to then seek out a coach, as I will describe. Professional coaches may find this process useful in their practices and in their lives.

I will also present an encapsulated step-by-step dyad model for coaching in pairs—the coach and the coachee. This model follows the basic outline of the generic model and also can be successfully transferred to couples, friends, teams, and larger groups, as I will show you.

After describing the in-depth generic Coaching by Values model and the brief CBV dyad model, I will provide examples of concrete action plans I use in corporate enterprises as part of Managing by Values (MBV). The

---

[73] If you prefer to do something more colorful and playful that is still part of CBV, I propose a card game that I designed to help convert every father and mother into a coach—not a professional coach, but rather one who can serve as a coach for his or her children and other family members. To learn more about it and order it, go to www.learning-about-values.com. When you receive it, just follow the enclosed instructions.

section of the chapter is geared to coaches, managers, and leaders. When engaging in culture reengineering in the corporate (for-profit or large nonprofit) world, even the professional coach may want to collaborate with a business consultant or a leader or manager in the organization who has been trained in transformational change.

Before we dive deeply into the CBV methodology, I should let you know that going through this process will take a while as it requires concentrated attention. If this is not a good time for you to do this, come back to it later. It will help you begin to answer the question, What is important in my life? In fact, even if you think you don't have time now, read just the first step; you might discover that you are so engaged you can't stop reading!

4.2 CBV methods for reengineering the business of life

CBV generic methodology

The generic Coaching by Values methodology is graphically displayed in Exhibit 4.1. There we can see the progression of the process.

Exhibit 4.1: Coaching by Values: The generic process

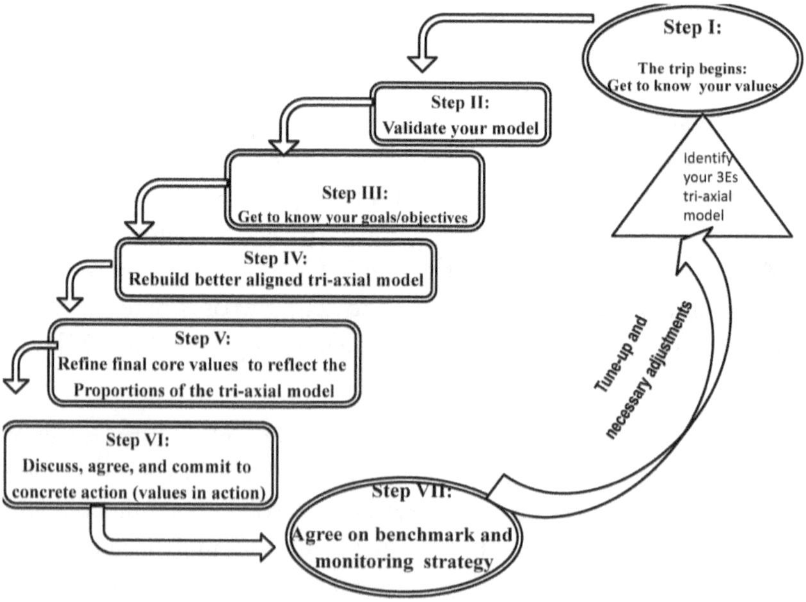

152

STEP I: Get to know your preferred values: The trip begins with or without a coach. The idea is to be involved in a process through which you get to know your preferred values. To do this, you need to do some brainstorming to identify preferred values. Then you need to answer the question, What is truly important to me in my life? This is a question that you will be asking throughout this generic process.

Step Ia. *List your values:* To make this task easier for you, my colleagues and I have put together an extensive list of values, which you'll find in Appendix 1. We suggest that you select 10 from the list of 60 possible values. Do not worry about the order of your list at this time. Just get everything down in writing. Remember we are talking about preferred, or *core,* values. If you are in the rush, the same exercise can be done by selecting only 5 values. Otherwise, the step-by-step methodology will become too complicated to manage.

You might end up with a list that looks something like this:

- health
- wealth
- playfulness
- happiness
- economic success
- care
- generosity
- adventure
- security
- empathy

There is no hard and fast rule for how long your list should be, but if it includes more than 5 to 10 values, consider shortening it. Are there some marginal values that just barely made your list? Consider cutting those. Or combine nearly identical values, like achievement/accomplishment.

Step Ib. *Attribute meaning, build initial tri-axial model of your values:* In previous chapters, we saw that there are different ways to analyze values. Here, I'm going to show you how to do this using the 3Es tri-axial model discussed in chapter 3. Begin by placing the values in your list in the three dimensions, or axes, of the model (for the sake of this discussion, we'll use the values in the list above):

> **economic-pragmatic:** wealth, economic success, security
> **social-ethical:** care, generosity
> **emotional-developmental:** health, playfulness, happiness, adventure, empathy

Next calculate each axis's percent of the whole, according to the number of values we've placed in it. We see that the economic-pragmatic axis, with four values, comprises 30% of the total values; the social-ethical, with two values, comprises 20%; and the emotional-developmental, with five values, comprises 50%. Using the tri-axial structure, we connect these points (3, 2, 5) on each axis to form a triangle (note that the point at which the axes intersect is not given a number and the first number on each axis is 0). This becomes the initial tri-axial model that is important in your life. It is graphically displayed in exhibit 4.2. In Appendix 2 is a template of the tri-axial model that you can use for repeated calculations.

Exhibit 4.2: Sample selected values represented proportionally in the 3Es tri-axial model

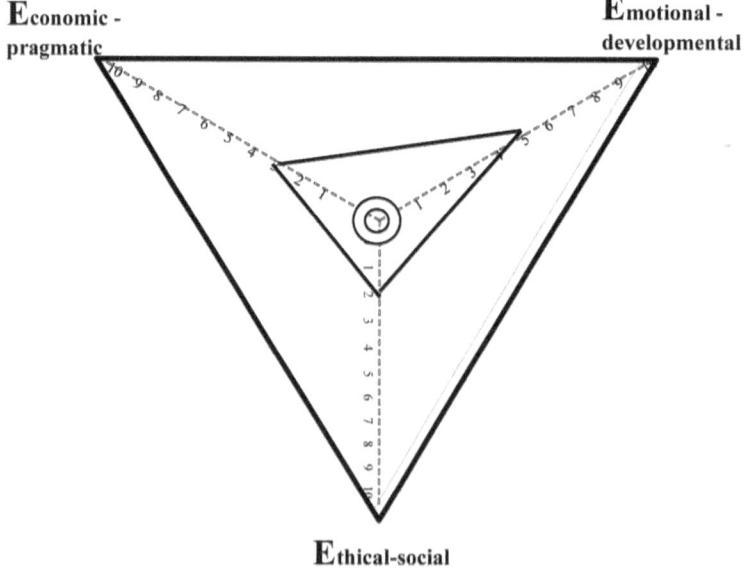

154

STEP II: Validation of the tri-axial model: Again, this step can be done with or without a coach. Look at your 3Es model and ask yourself, "What are my dominating values? Are they economic, ethical, or emotional?" If you are not satisfied with your answer, either change some values by swapping them out for others or assign new meaning to some of your originally selected values by reclassifying them—that is, by putting them in another family or dimension (axis). Now recalculate your tri-axial model. This analysis is very personal. No need to consult other people during the classification phase.

In this step, we see one of the beauties of the tri-axial structure. It gives you a visual way to begin to understand the "big picture." The number of values that fall in each axis (the percentage of your total values that each axis represents) shows you something essential about your life philosophy. What shape is the triangle? (Remember from chapter 2 that it will almost never be equilateral.) Which axis or axes dominate? Does one dominate in a way that seems disproportionate to you? Does this tell you something about yourself? Or does it not really reflect who you are? For example, you find that the values you chose in Step I fall mainly in the economic-pragmatic dimension, but you think of yourself as primarily an emotional, socially conscious person. Perhaps you'll want to chose new values more in sync with those dimensions. Or perhaps you will decide to reevaluate your sense of what is most important to you. As this process continues, you will revisit this again and again.

STEP III: Define (and refine) your goals and objectives: This phase may require a professional coach (e.g., a life coach), but it can be done independently. Your life goals should be things you would really like to accomplish. Maybe some things that you would love to attain and that you would be proud of.

***Step IIIa.** Define your goals:* No two people have identical life goals/objectives, so I can only suggest a few ideas. Basically you should look inside and see what your goals really are. Perhaps your life goals would look like this:

> **work:** to have a job that I am very good at, that matches my talents, and that I love
> **career:** to own my own company in the field in which I am most capable
> **money:** to become a millionaire

> **romantic**: to find a deep relationship with another person that is really fulfilling
>
> **creative:** to create something outstanding that is of great value to other people
>
> **social:** to contribute to and help other people as much as possible
>
> **spiritual:** to develop spiritually and to become a fully spiritually awake person

Step IIIb. *Refine your goals:* If you are not happy with your first list, change it. Refine it until you feel most comfortable, or satisfied, with it. This is a great opportunity to do some deep thinking about your goals. Go for it, keeping this in mind: Life goals can give you direction and success; they represent the experiences that you feel are part of the best life you could live. Not just a good life or even a great life; the *best* life. The idea is to develop an optimum level of goals without setting goals that are unrealistic. Very often, people select unrealistic goals and dedicate their entire lives to achieving the unachievable. These people usually end up paying with their health. They suffer from burnout and stress—and the life-threatening (and sometimes life-ending) conditions these can lead to.[74] One of the tasks of a life coach is to engage the coachee in discussions about what is real, what is achievable, and what goal(s) should be abandoned.

STEP IV: Rebuild a better aligned 3Es tri-axial model: Having gotten a broad understanding of the big picture through your work on Steps I, II, and III, you are ready to move to a more refined analysis and compare your values to your objectives and goals.

Step IVa. *Match your goals with your values:* The books and scholars that dominate the field of coaching suggest that that you derive your goals from your values. I recommend a more flexible approach—both deriving your values from your goals and your goals from your values. This is a more dynamic process. At a certain point, I realized that when I tried to use only the first approach, the result was a lot of frustration. I always felt I was missing something, because my static values list never seemed to

---

[74] See, for example: Dolan, S. L. (2006). *Stress, Self-Esteem, Health and Work*. Palgrave Macmillan; Dolan, S. L., & Moodie, S. (2010). Can becoming a manager be dangerous to your health? Is suicide the new occupational hazard? *Effective Executive*, 13(1), 66–69.

allow me to achieve certain goals. Eventually, I figured out that goals can be adjusted, and values can also be adapted to fit those goals; when a goal is reached, then a whole new values hierarchy can be created. In this step, rethink your values in light of the goals you identified above. Select the values that you believe will most help you achieve those goals.

As a university professor, I always wanted to achieve the goals of first getting tenure and then becoming a full professor. When I had achieved both goals, becoming one of the youngest full professors at the university where I taught, I realized the process of getting the tenure had not been congruent with my values of playfulness, creativity, and being an agent for social change. After receiving tenure, I decided to never again engage in projects that don't generate creativity, playfulness, and opportunities for social change, and I placed the economic-pragmatic values on the back burner, as their relative proportion in my 3Es model had been significantly diminished. This does not mean that I wouldn't have done all the hard work necessary to get tenure and become a full professor over again if I had the choice. This work allowed me to concentrate more effectively and enjoy more deeply the emotional-developmental and ethical-social values I'd put aside during that time. Now, I could re-embrace those values and bring them to the top of my hierarchy.

Step IVb. *Recalculate your tri-axial model to match your goals:* Select the final 3Es model that will make you happy. For the sake of this discussion, let us say its proportions are 60% emotional-developmental (EMO), 20% economic-pragmatic (ECO), and 20% ethical-social (ETH), which are different from those in Step I. Now do you see the problem with having a static list of values throughout your entire life? How is a single list of values going to allow you to be aligned with all your goals? The values that will make you a millionaire probably are not the same ones that will get you married. At some point in your life, however, you will need to focus intently on one of these goals while letting the others slide.

Although there will always be challenges and you may have some doubts, you need to get to the point in your evaluation that you are comfortable with the match between your 3Es model and your refined goal(s). The task of a coach is to help you achieve this.

STEP V: Refining your core values: The next step is to prioritize your individual list of core values and create your hierarchy of values. This is a time-consuming and difficult step because it requires some intense thinking. A coach can be instrumental in helping you reflect about the choices you will be making here. The core values you decide to use here should be limited to five, six, or seven. You may select them from your original list or choose values that were not included in that list. What is important is that you select these values in proportion to your corrected tri-axial model from the previous step.

Next, begin to construct a hierarchy of your values by asking yourself these questions: Which of these values is truly the most important to me in life? If I could only satisfy one of these values, which one would it be? The answer to this question is your number one value. Once you have identified the top value, move on to the second-highest value, and so on until you have sorted your values into a hierarchy from the top to the bottom.

Sometimes the highest priority value will be obvious to you. Other times you will have it narrowed down to a few choices but will have a hard time figuring out which one is really the most important among those. If that happens, try to be creative by inventing a scenario for each value, and then comparing those scenarios. An experienced coach can develop these scenarios for you if you need help.

For example, if you are trying to decide which is more important to you, health or wealth, ask yourself, Which would I rather do—exercise and spend my time traveling to a health foods or whole foods store to get healthy food or spend my time thinking about how to generate more money? This example assumes that exercising and making an effort to get healthy food would satisfy your value of health and that making an effort to engage in business opportunities would satisfy your value of accumulating more wealth, each to roughly the same degree. Create scenarios such as these, can help in the tough-to-prioritize values, the best ordering becomes clear.

So let us say we have sorted our list and respecting the proportions of the final tri-axial model in Step IV (60% EMO, 20% ECO, and 20% ETH), we have come up with the following priority list:

1. health (EMO)
2. playfulness (EMO)
3. happiness (EMO)
4. wealth (ECO)
5. care (ETH)

Getting to this point can tell you a lot about yourself. When you understand your values hierarchy, you should have a fair chance of predicting your behavior. The question is, of course, Do you really live (truly and honestly) your values? Do you, for example, make a constant daily effort to improve or maintain your health (first priority on your list)? Do you engage in situations permitting you to have fun (playfulness, second priority on your list)? Are you happy (third priority)? Do you take the necessary initiative and accomplish what you can to enhance your wealth (fourth priority)? Can you list ways in which you show care for others (your fifth priority)?

If you answered yes to these questions, you are experiencing value congruence: Your values are well aligned with your life. But if your core values, those that you've decided are the most important and meaningful to you, are not aligned with your daily life (are not realized in your behaviors), then you are living in a situation of misalignment, or incongruence. This, as we've seen, can take a heavy toll on your happiness and well-being. And to reverse this, so you can lead a more satisfying and healthier life, you will need a considered and thorough process of realignment.

STEP VI: Values in action: If you get to this step and congruence is apparent, you have reached the end the process. Your values seem to be aligned with your goals and objectives. You can always repeat this process in the future, and will probably want to, to ensure continuous alignment. But if your values are not aligned with your life, it is time to think about taking concrete behavioral measures (actions) to bring about congruence so that you are "walking the talk" and your behavior is consistent with your values.

When you decide to actually commit to change, it will help to a) form concrete plans (actions), b) define a time frame for accomplishing actions, and c) identify major challenges you will need to overcome. This can be done alone, but an experienced coach may make the process much easier by providing a variety of techniques, tools, and incentives for change and helping you establish your timetable. Most coaches work with a preferred methodology, ranging from the simple GROW model to the very nuanced and complex NPL, from Emotional Intelligence to Appreciative Inquiry. Some coaches are eclectic and employ a variety of techniques and approaches depending on the situation and the client. In chapter 1, I provided an overview of a few of these, to give you an idea of what is available. In the next section, I will show you some concrete action plans I use in the context of organizational change. Once you agree on specific actions, you need only start the change process. But to make sure you stay on course, you will want to put in place a monitoring plan.

STEP VII: Define the criteria for success and design monitoring follow-up: The final step is a) establishing a time frame for assessing your progress and tuning up your action plan if necessary, b) choosing benchmarks to meet along the way, and c) deciding on general criteria for success. A coach will clearly be helpful during this period.

CBV dyad process: A method for reengineering the business of life

The generic model described in the last section can be used by a single person without a coach. However, the process can be made easier and smoother with a coach's help. The following is an example of a coaching process that follows the general outline of the generic CBV model. In this example, the objective is to increase congruency between a coachee's values and her goals in her couple's relationship. It can be applied to any context—such as family, life, business, community—as I will describe later.

We will use the following symbols to represent the coach and the coachee:

☺ Coach

♀♂ Coachee

☺ **Step 1:** Coach provides a list of values

♀♂ **Step 2:** Coachee selects five or ten values from the list (see Appendix 1).

☺ ♀♂ **Step 3**: Coachee, with the help of the coach, builds an initial tri-axial model.

☺ ♀♂ **Step 4:** The coach and the coachee begin a dialogue to ensure that the model is valid. Coach and coachee correct the tri-axial model.

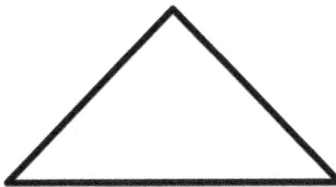

☺ ♀♂ **Step 5:** The coach and coachee discuss the meaning of success in a specific area of life or work (in this example, in her partner relationship). The coachee, with the help of the coach, defines her meaning of success in this relationship. This becomes the goal for the remainder of the coaching.

♀♂ **Step 6**: After a dialogue with the coach, the coachee selects five values reflecting her perception of her partner's primary values regarding the relationship. A tri-axial model is constructed based on these values. This is the partner's value model.

☺ ♀♂ **Step 7:** The coach and coachee compare the two tri-axial models. They identify and discuss congruences and incongruences. They craft action plans to reduce incongruence.

☺ ♀♂ **Step 8:** (after some time has passed) Coach and coachee discuss the experience and the actions the coachee has taken. They address problems she's encountered, agree on steps to realignment, and tune up her action plans.

Applying CBV dyad process to larger groups

With some slight modifications, we can apply the same methodology to larger coaching contexts, such as couples coaching, family coaching, and coaching a team or even larger unit. First, the coach works with both partners in the couple or all members of the team together, facilitating group discussions and the building of tri-axial models. After they define and establish overall goals, the coach works with members individually in dyad relationships.

Here are some suggestions for arriving at a diagnosis and crafting a strategy of alignment ("team" in the following can be a couple, family, group, or other system):

- Coach conducts a value audit of each member of the team.

- Each member of the team builds his or her own tri-axial model based on his own preferred values.

- Team discusses current state and identifies values manifested in current team culture.

- Based on values detected in previous step, team develops an aggregate team culture tri-axial model. This tri-axial model represents the current *real* culture in the team.

- Members of the team begin a dialogue based on the tri-axial model above. They identify gaps between their own models and group model. They discuss the direction they'd like the group to go in and define success in the team. They agree on a final desired culture. This culture embeds the definition of success. Team selects five, six, or seven core values based on consensus.

- A coach works individually in a dyad relationship with each member of the team to help develop a strategy of value alignment. This can be done in a group if the coach has the skills to do the work with multiple coachees at the same time.

- The team, with coach, discusses plans to reinforce and preserve the agreed-upon reengineered culture.

- Together they plan future monitoring, benchmarks, and tune-up.

Exhibit 4.3: An example of work team diagnosis (n=14 members)

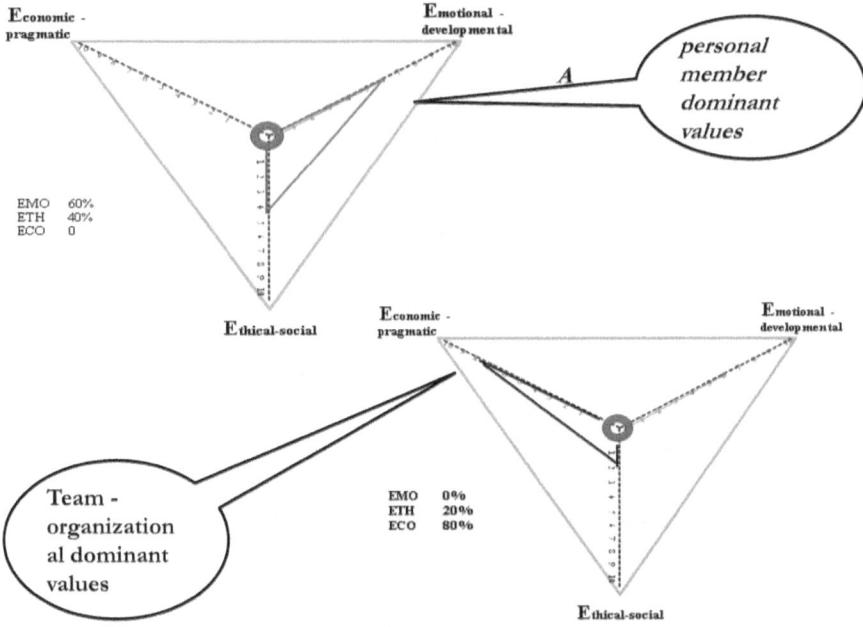

The diagnosis shows that the dominant personal values are emotional-developmental (60%), followed by ethical-social (40%), with no economic-pragmatic values. The reality in the workplace is remarkable—and remarkably different from the values of the team members. There is an 80% domination of economic-pragmatic values, followed by 20% ethical-social values, and *zero* emotional-developmental values. Although the team members individually like and enjoy passion and emotion, they are working in a culture that does not offer opportunities for their expression.

4.3 The Gift of Values: A coaching enrichment module

Have you ever wondered what those gifts that you are either giving or receiving mean? A lot of people may not think about it and just buy anything as long as they have something to give. But every gift has a meaning, especially to those who are really close and value their relationship a lot. Often, the monetary value of the gift is not relevant; it's the meaning that is more important. Christmas cards and birthday cards that you make yourself can be more meaningful than any expensive gifts.

Gifts can convey thoughts, feelings, and sentiments without words. Even cards are sometimes only graphical; they may contain no words, but the meaning behind them is clear. Actions, such as helping someone build a garden or bringing soup to a sick friend, can also be gifts. Gifts symbolize expressions or feelings that are sometimes better shown through actions. Some of the expressions that gifts convey are the following:

- expression of love or friendship

- expression of gratitude for a gift received or favor

- expression of piety (in the form of charity)

- expression of solidarity (in the form of mutual aid)

What is the Gift of Values? The Gift of Values is a form for a person to suggest (give) a value that they would like to see the coachee using in his or her daily life. This can become part of a methodology used by a coach, a partner, a work team colleague, or other close person as feedback and food for thought; it can solidify the tri-axial model, help increase alignment over the long run, and be an important element of the coaching process.

How does it work? After the coachee has built his or her tri-axial model, it can be very important for him to understand how another person sees his values in action (behavior) and to understand what the other person expects him to exhibit given his espoused values.

A coach can ask a person, "Now that I understand your values, will you be willing to accept a gift from me? Here is the value that I am proposing." This new value can change the proportions of the tri-axial model. It can be very powerful for a couple when they are attempting to align their values. Because this gift comes from someone that one cares about (e.g., a partner, a colleague, a coach), the recipient will consider it seriously and likely be willing to incorporate the gift into his or her 3Es tri-axial model.

I use the Gift of Values very often in my coaching sessions, and the results are outstanding; it makes the coachee aware of personal blind spots and shortcomings. It is one more step in reshaping and aligning the coachee's tri-axial model, and the coachee can consider incorporating the gift into his or her final core values.

4.4 CBV processes, methods, tools for reengineering the life of business

Before presenting the processes and methodologies in this section, I should add that they are likely beyond the knowledge and skill set of a traditional coach. They require an understanding of the dynamics of organizational change, including mechanisms and strategies to overcome resistance to change, so a coach will want to collaborate with an organizational consultant or transformational leader within the organization.

Culture reengineering

To survive in the twenty-first century, companies will have to develop a new way to operate, a new culture. But changing the organizational culture is the toughest task managers or any organizational consultant (including a coach) may face. The organizational culture was formed over years of interaction among the participants in the organization. Changing the culture may be a problem either because the leaders of the organization do not see the need to change it, or because they do not have the competences to manage the change.

In a most interesting article published in the *European Business Forum*, J. Sheth and R. Sisodia attribute the increase in organizations that disappear—even those with a history of success are failing in greater numbers—to two principal causes: leadership's inability to change and leadership's unwillingness to do so.[75] Both leaders who do not have the competency and those who do not have the courage to engage in transforming their organizations and adapting to an increasingly complex environment are doomed to create the most stressful situation for their stakeholders: extinction. Exhibit 4.4 presents the leadership options and the organizational states resulting from their attitudes, as I explain below.

Exhibit 4.4: Leadership willingness and ability to change

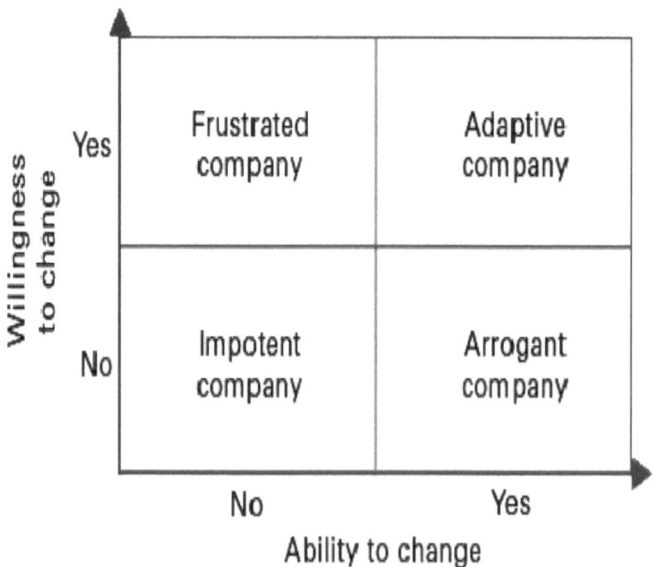

---

[75]   Sheth, J., & Sisodia, R. (2005). Why good companies fail? European Business Forum, 22, 24–31.

- **Frustrated companies** (and frustrated employees) occur when their leadership is willing to change but does not have the ability to. Usually such leaders do not have the skills and competencies to manage large-scale changes; they do not know how to forge alliances or overcome resistance to change.

- **Arrogant companies** have leaders who are able to change but are unwilling to because of myopia, orthodoxies based on their past success, and the belief that they, and only they, know what is best for the company. When executives or organizations succeed by accident, they often become very rigid about their belief systems, much more rigid than they were before becoming successful. In a way, they become superstitious. They end up believing that they will succeed forever, and then they become resistant to change. Employees in these types of corporations are highly stressed. Leaders falling into this category must continually identify and battle their own orthodoxies, which are often disguised as strengths but are, in fact, vulnerabilities.

- **Impotent companies** are those whose leaders are neither willing nor able to change, and are therefore doomed to obsolescence.

- **Adaptive companies** are those which their leaders are willing and able to change as needed. These are the companies that will survive and thrive in the long run. These are the type of leaders who may understand the benefits of constantly evaluating their mission, vision, and respective culture and assure an alliance among them.

Consequently, culture reengineering is a top-down approach. In the first step, the coach must make sure that the organization has transformational leaders and that a good value (culture) audit had been carried out so that the current situation is clear. When leaders recognize that their current organizational culture needs to transform to ensure continuation of the organization's success and progress, change can occur. But change is not pretty and change is not easy. The good news, however, is that organizational culture change is possible. It requires understanding, commitment, and tools.

Managing the process step-by-step

This Managing by Values process for organizational change is similar to the process I described earlier for value reengineering for a single person, except many more people are involved and the process is much more complex. Exhibit 4.5 shows basic steps of the organizational culture change process.

Pre Phase: Set the conditions for change and conducting value/ culture audit: In the book *Managing by Values,* which I coauthored with Salvador Garcia and Bonnie Richley, we called this "Phase 0" because it is an essential prerequisite, a sine qua non for the whole process.[76] Many projects of strategic revitalization of the ways of thinking and doing things in an organization turn out to be mere intentions—sometimes even pseudo-intentions—not founded on solid arguments or rationale or funded with adequate resources. In other words, *good intentions are not enough for the management of change.* The fate of the initial phase of implementing culture change resides with the answers to the following questions:

- Is the organization serious about a culture change?

- Is the organization ready to engage in a long-term action? How is "long-term" defined?

- Does the organization have the right type of leadership to initiate and sustain the process?

- Does the organization have the necessary resources? What resources will are those?

A negative, or even tentative, response to the questions indicates that more thought, time, and discussion should take place before attempting

---

[76] Dolan, S. L., Garcia, S., & Richley, B. (2006). *Managing by Values: Corporate Guide to Living, Being Alive and Making a Living in the 21st Century.* London: Palgrave Macmillan.

to implement a culture change. The key to a successful change process is dependent on (more than any other factor) the presence of one or more true leaders who can legitimize the process by demonstrating the will, commitment, and capability to deploy all the necessary resources. Regrettably, experience shows that this make-or-break condition is not all that frequently met and is the reason for many culture change failures.

Another component of the pre-change conditions is an organization-wide culture (values) audit. Different culture audits exist and vary depending on the conceptual model used in measuring the culture (see, for example, the vignette in this chapter by Richard Barrett). The MBV Audit[77] is a concept and a tool for measuring the values of the core stakeholders (employees) and comparing them with the values of the organization. When analysis reveals differences between personal values and needs and those of the organization, the need to reengineer the culture becomes critical.

Exhibit 4.5: Step-by-step culture reengineering methodology

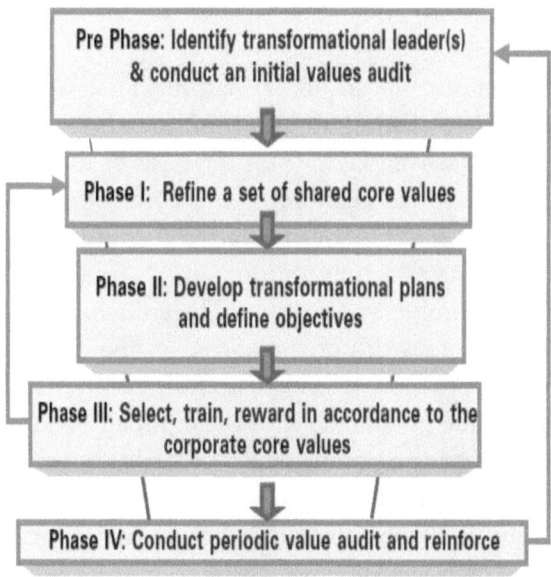

---

[77] For a demonstration and more information, go to www.MBVsuite.com. Select "English" (or whichever language you want) from the dropdown menu in the top right-hand corner.

Phase I: Distill the essential values: Once the political will to change is confirmed as a serious intention, and resources are in place to allocate the resources required, the first phase of work on the culture reengineering consists of reformulating values, with the maximum participation at all levels. There are three basic sequential activities for this first phase of an MBV project:

1. Collective visualization of the kind of future desired, described and expressed as the final values to be incorporated in the organization's vision and mission

2. Participation in the diagnosis of the strengths and weaknesses of the organization's current set of values and how these measure up against the opportunities and threats of the organization's environment

3. Building a consensus on the lines to be followed in the path to change (new operating values to constitute the ruling culture of the organization)

This distillation of propositions, situational analyses, and rules of the game that command common and enthusiastic support may be seen as the generation of a massive dialogue on the basis of the values and shared perspectives of as many as possible of the committed members of the organization, including the associated interest groups such as the main suppliers and customers, trades unions, and professional associations. Involve as many stakeholders as possible. The guidelines to the distillation process will be the framework of the agreed proportion of values in the economic-pragmatic, the ethical-social, and the emotional-developmental dimensions and will be in alliance with the company vision and mission.

The idea of involving as many stakeholders as possible in the design of a new culture may seem totally utopian, but it is logically inescapable if you hope to create an environment based on shared values. Managing by Values recognizes the potential of everyone to make a contribution based on their knowledge and experience and understands that mutual learning is not constrained by notions of up, down or sideways, in a dynamic and open organization.

At the beginning of the twenty-first century, some business leaders are timidly beginning to consider a new organizational configuration for thinking and behaving at work: a new culture that breaks with the old, arrogant supposition that only those at the top have "the answers," have the knowledge, experience, and energy to design and implement the strategies for survival and prosperity in the future. It is gradually being accepted that predictions and prescriptions by experts—even internal ones—are not as valid or effective as the creative visions shared by all. The stimulation of entrepreneurial initiative and behavior propounded by writers on "excellent companies" is increasingly recognized as vitally important for competitiveness, and few can muster convincing arguments against it.

A participative process of internal dialogue should begin at the organization at all levels with the aim of reformulating the organization's essential operating values. A task force needs to be created to manage this dialogue. At the end of the process, limited (or distilled) values should be chosen. As a general guide, the company should select and define its values from the CBV tri-axial model's three dimensions (as discussed in chapter 2 and earlier in this chapter): (1) economic-pragmatic values; (2) ethical-social values; and (3) emotional-developmental. If values from all three of these areas are not included, the "new" culture will likely not be very new at all, and the lopsided foundation will result in a failed change effort.

Phase II: We are actually changing! It's time to put the project teams to work: The work in Phase I began to make changes in the organization's way of thinking and doing things. The inclusive nature of the process alone has likely established a basis for the employees' engagement in the transformed culture, by creating trust and a renewed sense of belonging. Thus, working attitudes have already begun to change. Now the newly defined shared core operating values must be concretely translated into changes in everyday work processes and work tasks. When an organization has an inspiring vision, a meaningful mission, and a workable culture "enshrined" in a good set of agreed-upon operating values, it is ready to define its principal lines of action in terms of a properly thought-out structure for achieving long-, medium-, and short-term objectives. This is best organized through project teams and it should include processes that ensure a flexible, dynamic culture.

Phase III: Design human resource policies based on values: The internal policies related to human resource policies (for example selection, training, promotion, incentives, evaluation, and the like) in most companies normally suffer from two basic characteristics:

1. They are not sufficiently coherent in their relationship to the strategy formally followed by the senior management.

2. They are not appropriately articulated nor are they integrated as a function of any type of model or strong ruling idea.

As a result, they are developed in a fragmented way and thus lose their capacity to reinforce each other. All the values identified by the company as essential for its success should be strengthened by means of training interventions. How is it possible, for example, for any company to adopt a strategy of innovation without establishing a basic training program in techniques of creativity throughout all the functional areas of the organization? Probably, leaders of more than half the companies in any industry in any country would claim to be following a strategy of innovation, but if these strategies do not include effective, inspiring, and energizing training, the leaders will never see the imaginative or groundbreaking innovations they were expecting.

Being effective at modifying and strengthening personal values is one of the most interesting and rewarding training objectives one could aspire to. It is challenging on a professional level because it must be approached with exquisite respect for individual integrity and liberty of thought and expression. It is in this phase that reward systems and promotion criteria should also be evaluated and reinvented.

Phase IV: Monitor operational values via culture audits: The most frequent and regrettable error company leaders can make after they think they have successfully reformulated the vision, mission, and operating values of their company is publishing them in an attractive format—and then *doing absolutely nothing* to evaluate and reward employees' assimilation and compliance with the new culture. In Phase II, I discussed the importance of converting the shared values into action objectives that are directly relevant to everyday work processes. These action objectives not only should be reinforced through rewards and incentives as we discussed in the last step, they should be capable of measurement. The essential architecture of a planned culture change rests on two pillars: the implementation of the change process (i.e., crafting it and putting it into practice) and the maintenance of its sustainability through ongoing evaluation.

The successful adoption of a new culture requires that it be dynamic, with an organization-wide commitment to continuous learning and continuous improvement, periodical reviews of values, mechanisms in place for articulating and instilling the shared values of the vibrant new culture in actions and in words, and procedures for recruiting new employees who are eager to share these values. The continued strength and growth of the new culture requires a process of auditing to monitor progress and to ensure that everyone is actually doing what they have said they will do. This auditing process must be subject to the same conditions as the change process that generated the new culture: It must be all-inclusive, with no levels and no areas free from scrutiny. It must be open. It must be undertaken professionally and sympathetically, not as a threat if deficiencies are revealed but as an opportunity for resolving misunderstandings, compensating for unexpected problems, and allocating more resources if underestimations were made.

Finally, underlying all audits as well as all phases of the change process must be a recognition and acknowledgement that values of the employees need to be aligned with the vision and the mission of the company. The Coaching by Values tri-axial model is an excellent tool to diagnose value gaps and to reengage members at any level of an organization. It can be used at any time—from the start of the change process throughout its implementation and auditing. As I said in chapter 3, leaving an organization is not always a bad thing. When disconnects are detected or suspected, the tri-axial model can help determine if adjustment is possible—either by the organization or any member at any level. The process of reengineering is a continuous process, one that can allow an organization to grow and thrive as the world presents evermore complex challenges.

As it progresses, keep in mind the Coaching by Values philosophy: alignment between shared core values, the organization's mission, and its future vision.

The need for culture audit: The case of mergers and acquisitions

Mergers and acquisitions are becoming a normal way to do business and expand in the twenty-first century. The value of global mergers and acquisitions in 2010 was (USD) $2.4 trillion, and it is expected to grow during 2011.[78] But despite the time and money invested in mergers and acquisitions deals, many failed. Recent studies estimate the failure rate of mergers at close to 75%. This statistic raises the question, Why do so many mergers and acquisitions fail to achieve their intended results?

The high failure rate has less to do with paying too high a purchase price or making a poor strategic fit than one would think. Rather, many failed organizational marriages are the result of companies having failed to critically examine the possible ramifications of their cultural differences on post-combination success. Just as two individuals with differing values and beliefs will not co-exist for long, unsuitable organizational marriages won't last. Thus, many companies include cultural assessment as part of their due diligence to discern, prior to the altar, if the cultural differences can be managed post-merger.

Because culture represents shared beliefs, assumptions, and values, it is not readily observable. An organization's culture often only becomes obvious when contrasted with the culture of another organization, such as in the case of the merger of two firms. When two organizations unite, the combination inevitably results in some form of culture shock. The extent of culture shock can range from slightly unpleasant to exceptionally distressing, depending on how employees in each organization evaluate the attractiveness of the other culture in regard to their own. Generally, the greater the cultural dissimilarity, the greater the culture shock. Culture clashes can be the result of several factors, including ignorance (i.e., lack

---

[78] Data furnished by Y. Weber, world expert on mergers and acquisitions. For some of his recent work in this field, see: Weber, Y., & Drori, I. (2011, forthcoming). Integrating organizational and human behavior perspectives on mergers and acquisitions: looking inside the black box. *International Studies of Management and Organizations*; Weber, Y., Teerkangas, S, Rouzies, A., & Tarba, S. (2011, forthcoming). Cross-cultural management in mergers and acquisitions. *European Journal of International Management.*

of understanding of another's culture), disrespect for another company's norms, and arrogance (i.e., a belief that one culture is superior).

Though a seemingly innocent misunderstanding, such occurrences frequently result in failed organizational marriages. Consequently, companies have begun to acknowledge the existence of divergent cultures, identify cultural components that potentially hinder successful combination, and prioritize the cultural dimensions believed to be most important for a successful combination. This process of analyzing the fit between two independent organizations is known as cultural due diligence.

Until very recently, there were no systematic tools for performing cultural due diligence. There was no overall conceptual model, let alone a defined process and analytical tools. The tri-axial model and the Managing by Values methodology fill this gap. They can be applied at any stage of the merger or acquisition to provide data that can help managers decide to move forward with a merger, anticipate significant problems as the merger is completed, and deal effectively with problems post-merger.

Cultural audits help to determine the extent to which a company's current culture aligns with the type of culture required for success in the future. When done properly, information from a cultural audit will highlight similarities, and significant differences, between the cultures in question. Cultural disparities, even those that are significant, do not necessarily jeopardize merger and acquisition activities. In many instances it is precisely the cultural difference that attracts companies to one another. Nonetheless, it is imperative that those involved in merger and acquisition discussions have reliable information at their disposal regarding cultural similarities and differences so they can make informed decisions on how to best combine the cultures

A cultural due diligence technique provides an operational framework for managing cultural differences by uncovering potential pitfalls and their implications prior to completing a deal. Though cultural due diligence often uncovers significant differences in organizational practices among merging companies, the intent of the process is not to discourage integration. Rather, cultural due diligence is meant to alert stakeholders to potential differences in the human side of the merger equation so that plans to manage these disparities can be developed. In some instances, cultural differences may be too intransigent to bridge. However, with information derived from a cultural audit, decision-makers can systematically address potential hazards and take the necessary steps to overcome them before they severely impede the transition.

Implementation of value alignment in a large insurance company

In this section, I will briefly describe a typical process of culture reengineering, or value alignment. This is a real case, but for reasons of confidentiality I can not reveal the name of the company. The case involves a large insurance company in a former Soviet-bloc Eastern European country. The company went from being state-run to private and struggled to educate its employees about competitive private sector values. It had been private for about 15 years before our intervention, and given its size and market share, the company had been very profitable. Recently, it had gone through structural changes due to its acquisition by a large U.K.-based insurance company. It is now part of a global operation.

The situation: The management team in the company (we'll call it "the Insurance Company") attempted to develop programs for value sharing and value alignment over the past two years, but results were not satisfactory. Although values were identified, indicators seem to suggest that they were neither shared nor aligned with the vision of the company. A recent survey pointed out that a large percentage of the employees work under stress and feel stressful. As an added difficulty, a large multinational corporation (MNC) based in London had acquired the company. The MNC attempted to standardize its operation worldwide and introduced a management model based on principles of action that did not match the culture and values of the Insurance Company.

Objective of the value alignment intervention: The development and implementation of a hybrid model of value alignment that uses the MNC head office principles in conjunction with the local values of the Insurance Company, and move to set up methodologies, policies, and practices that will facilitate shared and sustainable alignment of the newly developed hybrid model.

Methodology: Project run jointly by a team of external consultants and a team selected by the Insurance Company. The joint team constitutes the culture reengineering task force and is responsible for all phases of the diagnosis, development, and implementation of the project. The methodology is described in exhibit 4.6

Exhibit 4.6: Process overview

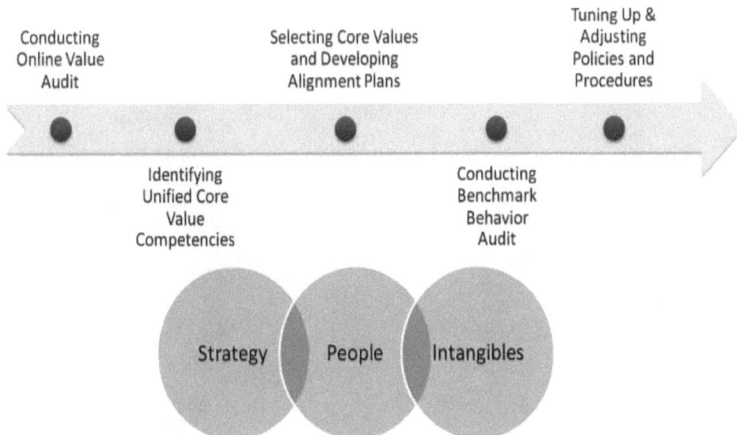

Benchmark of principal phases for the implementation included the following:

- creation of a joint task force (training if needed)
- development of an action plan and benchmark timetable
- translation of value questionnaire to local language (validation)
- online questionnaire, data collection, and analysis (production of a report)
- development of alignments plans (hybrid model)
- implementation of plans (division of labor, revising hr policies connected, others)
- behavior audit, monitoring and adjustment of sustainable plans
- end of the project

After the completion of the process, the Insurance Company was interested in adding an individual change management program. We proposed an expanded Coaching by Values framework, which (see exhibit 4.7) includes programs for stress management and work-life balance. Coaching can work very well (hand in hand) with these additional modules.

Exhibit 4.7: Enhanced Coaching by Values model for promoting wellness

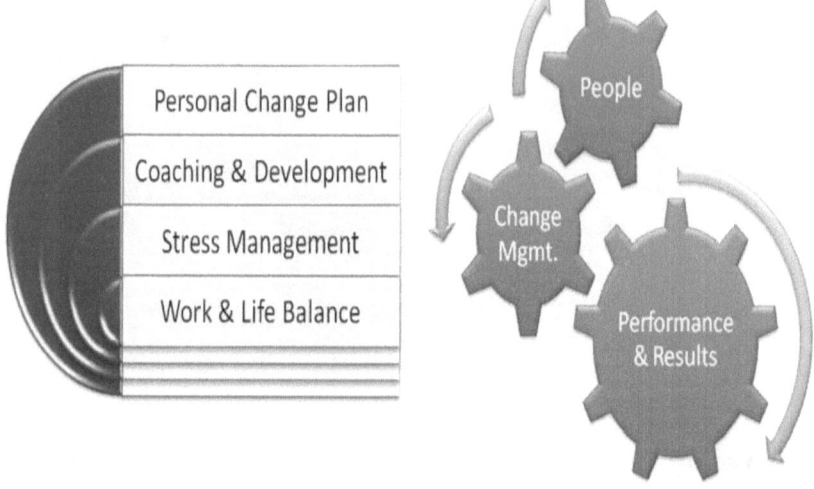

Tools for Coaching: Measuring Consciousness by Mapping Values

Richard Barrett

Values and levels of consciousness

Every value you can think of belongs to a level of consciousness. Therefore, the values that are important to you at any point in your life reflect the state of evolution of your consciousness. By mapping your values, you can determine the levels of consciousness you are operating from.

The model we use at the Barrett Values Centre (www.valuescentre. com) to measure consciousness consists of three stages and seven levels. The first stage, which contains three levels, is about satisfying the needs of the ego by learning how to become viable and independent in your framework of existence. Level 1 is about meeting your basic survival needs. Level 2 is about belonging and meeting your relationship needs. Level 3 is about differentiation and meeting your self-esteem needs. During this stage of evolution you are primarily focused on satisfying the needs of the ego: values such as financial stability, belonging, respect, recognition, and the like. Whenever the ego gets fearful about being able to get its needs met, you display negative or potentially limiting values, such as jealousy, blame, manipulation, and arrogance.

The second stage, which contains two levels, is about learning to blend the needs of the ego with the needs of the soul so you can become an authentic individual. Level 4 is about individuation, becoming more fully who you are by facing and overcoming your fears. Level 5 is about self-actualization—aligning your work in the world with your passion (soul purpose).

The third stage, which also contains two levels, is about learning how to align and cooperate with other individuals to achieve personal fulfillment. Level 6 is about actualizing your own sense of purpose and at the same time aligning with others who share a similar purpose to make a difference in the world. When you are fully aligned with your purpose and making a difference becomes a way of life, you reach level 7, the level of service.

When you are able to overcome your fears and master each level of consciousness through the display of positive values, you attain full-spectrum consciousness. The New Leadership Paradigm book, website, and learning system (www.newleadershipparadigm.com) provide a full account of this process. The learning system includes a downloadable learning module consisting of 43 exercises that can be used by coaches for supporting their clients in learning to lead themselves and become full-spectrum individuals. The learning module also includes a journal and self-evaluation tools whereby individuals can record their progress on their self-leadership journey. In addition to the Leading Self learning module, there are modules for Leading a Team, Leading an Organization, and Leading in Society.

Cultural transformation tools

In addition to the exercises included in the Leading Self learning module, the Barrett Values Centre has developed a series of assessments for measuring the consciousness of individuals, organizations, and nations. Three of these instruments are used extensively by coaches to support their clients in their personal and professional evolution.

The Individual Values Assessment

The Individual Values Assessment is a self-assessment instrument that enables you to measure how aligned you are with the culture and values of your organization; how well you connect with your organization and the work you do; and to what extent you think your organization is on the right track. The insights gained from this instrument are crucial to understanding to what extent you believe you will be able to find the fulfillment you are looking for in your present job.

The Leadership Values Assessment

Individuals only grow and develop when they get regular feedback. The Leadership Values Assessment compares a leader's perception of his or her operating style with the perception of his or her superiors, peers, and subordinates. It enables you to find out what others appreciate about you; what advice your superiors, peers, and subordinates can offer you to improve your leadership style; what levels of consciousness you operate from; and your level of personal dysfunction—the extent to which you are operating from the fears of your ego. The debrief of the Leadership Values Assessment is rich in feedback and usually takes about two to three hours.

The Leadership Development Report

The Leadership Development Report, like the Leadership Values Assessment, is a powerful coaching tool for promoting self-awareness, personal transformation, and an understanding of the actions a leader needs to take to realize his or her full potential. The Leadership Development Report also compares a leader's perception of his or her operating style with the perception of his or her superiors, peers, and subordinates. Assessors also get the opportunity to indicate how they believe the leader needs to change to help him or her become the best leader he or she can be. Emphasis is placed on a leader's strengths, areas for improvement, and opportunities for growth.

There are three main differences between the Leadership Development Report and the Leadership Values Assessment. First, the Leadership Development Report asks the assessors to rate the leader against a prescribed set of 26 full spectrum "behaviors" that our research has shown to be significant. The Leadership Values Assessment, on the other hand, allows assessors to write freeform responses to questions about the leader's strengths and areas for improvement. Second, the Leadership Development Report delivers a fully automated report, whereas the Leadership Values Assessment is handwritten by one of our analysts. Third, the Leadership Development Report uses a standard template of values, whereas Leadership Values Assessment template is customized to reflect the cultural attributes of your organization.

RICHARD BARRETT

Richard Barrett is the founder and chairman of the Barrett Values Centre. He is an internationally recognized author, consultant, and keynote speaker on values-based leadership and culture in business business and society. He is a visiting lecturer at the Consulting and Coaching for Change, leadership course run jointly by HEC Executive Education in Paris and the Saïd Business School, University of Oxford. He is also an adjunct professor at Royal Roads University, Institute for Values-Based Leadership. Barrett is the author of *A Guide to Liberating Your Soul (1995), Liberating the Corporate Soul: Building a Visionary Organization (1998), Building a Values-Driven Organization: A Whole System Approach to Cultural Transformation (2006), and The New Leadership Paradigm* (2011). E-mail: richard@valuescentre. com. Web: www.valuescentre.com; www.newleadershipparadigm.com; and www.valuesjournal.com.

Conclusion

This chapter is the crystallization of my Coaching by Values ideas and methodologies to this point. I hope that you are still with me. I know this chapter may have been a bit difficult to read (it was certainly difficult for me to write!), but now that you appreciate the CBV ideas and have a handle on the overall CBV process—that is, you are clear about what each step is, how it arose from the previous step, and how it progresses to the next—there is no limit to where you can go.

A coach can be eclectic. You may want to draw from other coaching schools at various points in an intervention to help achieve your primary goal of effecting change. Follow the steps in the sequence I've described, but within those steps, be creative. Enrich the experience. An example of enrichment that I use is the Gift of Values that I described here. Be imaginative.

This is not the end of the story. In the next chapter, I imagine what might happen to our world and how CBV methods may grow in the future in response to opportunities presenting themselves and challenges confronting us right now.

CBV Reflection ♣ ♠ ♥

Think of the key message(s) you retained after reading this chapter. Then complete the following sentences:

The principal points I liked in this chapter include

1._____

2._____

3._____

The principal points that I did not like or disagreed with in this chapter include

1._____

2._____

3._____

Chapter 5

Toward a Universal and Future-Oriented Model of World Values

- 5.1 Introduction

- 5.2 The neurobiology of values

- 5.3 Values and spirituality: The inner voyage to coaching

- 5.4 Values in the New Age (new global needs and new paradigms)

- Conclusion

5.1 Introduction

If you have read the first four chapters in this book mindfully—and if I have done my job—you are really familiar with the concept, methodology, and tools of Coaching by Values, and you are equipped to apply them in whatever settings you find suitable. This chapter is a bonus chapter. It is for those who wish to have a go at the future. This chapter is somewhat speculative; more research is needed (and is being carried out) to substantiate some of what I discuss here. Look at it as an appetizer, a few suggestions of what may come to pass (or not) in the future.

In this chapter I explore—and at times envision possible future developments in—areas ranging from the neurobiology of values to spirituality and New Age values. I propose extending the tri-axial model into a quad-axial model for use in leadership. I imagine how some New Age values may help us resolve the global challenges the world is facing. I do not claim that my discussion of any of these areas is complete; that would take many books by many authors. I do, however, want to share with you some issues that I will most likely address in more depth in a future edition of this book.

Values, Managing by Values, and Coaching by Values are dynamic concepts and methodologies. They have evolved dramatically since I first began my journey with them in 1997. And they will continue to evolve. It is part of their nature. If you are creative and innovative, you may decide not to wait for the future, but to integrate some of the ideas I speculate about here into the methodology I presented earlier.

5.2 The neurobiology of values

How do humans develop the values that permit us to classify objects as beautiful or ugly and to judge actions as good or evil? Where are good social conduct and ethical principles grounded? We have long been preoccupied with such questions. Some of the answers may be found in our evolution, specifically in our neurobiology. Recent research suggests that the evolution of human values may be imprinted in the human brain, both in its gross anatomy and in the finer details of its physiology, including brain chemistry. Developments in neuroscience indicate that values evolved as the human brain did, with each affecting the other.

Humans have been pondering the origins of their values for centuries. Until recent times, such issues were primarily the province of philosophers, theologians, sociologists, and historians who studied the universality of or variations in specific values across different cultures. Neuroscience and other scientific disciplines are making a more objective and experimental approach possible. The imaging techniques used to display the living brain, for example, allow us to see which areas of the brain are activated when people are manifesting different classes of values. And because the field of neuroscience is expanding to include neurophysiology, neurology, and anatomy, among other areas of science, more tools will likely be available soon to further our understanding of this complicated, vexing, and wonderful issue.

In recent years, several concrete observations have laid the foundation for a neuroscience of values. Brain images of people responding to questionnaires designed to evaluate moral and ethical attitudes show clearly that certain attitudes are associated with certain parts of the brain. We have also learned that specific neurons or neural networks are involved when a person is displaying a sense of empathy. Data from some brain imaging studies suggest not only that there is a cerebral substance connected with values associated with empathy, but also that it developed by evolutionary selection.

One proposed explanation is that the biological blueprint of human values stems from the "life regulation system," which is known as homeostasis. All life forms have systems that permit them to maintain biological processes within a range compatible with life. In complex species (like the human), the regulation of life depends on a close interaction between brain systems and body-proper systems and is controlled in effect by specific collection of well-coordinated brain regions. Life regulation is not automatic; it involves choices and preferences, but at the most basic levels those choices and preferences are made subconsciously. The life regulation system, or homeostasis, is built to achieve certain goals, among them the maintenance of health, the prevention of circumstances leading to death, and the procurement of states of life tending toward optimal function rather than merely neutral or defective function.

Homeostasis inherently embodies values in the sense that it rejects certain conditions of operation, those that would lead to disease or death, and seeks conditions that lead to optimal survival. Therefore, one can claim that what we call "good" and "evil" are aligned with categories of actions related to particular ranges of homeostatic regulation. What we call good actions are, in general, those actions that lead to health and well-being in an individual, a group, or an entire community. What we call evil, on the other hand, pertains to malaise, disease, or death in the individual, the group, or the community.

The same can apply to other values, such as efficiency or inefficiency. The inefficient part of the regulatory spectrum is characterized by higher energy consumption, inadequate performance, impediments, and the like. At the dawn of the human values, we presume, objects that were classified as beautiful were associated with efficient states, either because they occurred in life circumstances in which the homeostatic range was efficient or because the objects themselves were capable of causing efficient homeostatic states.[79]

Throughout this book, I have insisted that social and relational life is strongly linked to beliefs, values, and attitudes, which are themselves governed by an anatomical substance. This has been studied using brain imaging techniques. Davidson[80] found that activity in the ventromedial prefrontal cortices of the brain (VMPEC) is greatest in people who are very compassionate and caring. His work also showed the remarkable heterogeneity among individuals in their affective style and values. Viewing Davidson's work in light of the homeostatic theory of values, one can hypothesize that human values evolved along with the species to ensure maximum survival and that these values in turn may have caused cerebral modifications. Is there a relationship between changes in the human frontal brain areas and the emergence of values? A variety of scientific evidence confirms the existence of a neural network that is activated during the exercise of some values (moral, ethical). This network links the prefrontal and medial temporal lobes.

Throughout its evolution, the human brain has acquired three components that progressively appeared and grew one on top of the other, similar to strata in an archeological site: the oldest (the archipallium or primitive) is located at the bottom and to the back; the next one (the paleopallium) is in an intermediate position; the most recent (the neopallium,

---

[79] See Damasio, A. (pp. 47–56) in: Changeux, J. P., Damasio, A., & Singer, W. J. (Eds.). (2005). *Neurobiology of Human Values*. Springer.

[80] See Davidson, R.J. (pp. 67–90) in: Changeux, J. P., Damasio, A., & Singer, W. J. (Eds.). (2005). *Neurobiology of Human Values*. Springer.

also known as the superior or rational) is situated on top and to the front. These are like three biological computers that although interconnected retain their particular types of intelligence, subjectivity, sense of time and space, memory, mobility, and other less specific functions.

In 1878, the French neurologist Paul Broca called attention to the fact that, on the medial surface of the mammalian brain, right underneath the cortex, is an area containing several nuclei of gray matter (neurons) that he called the "limbic lobe" (from the Latin word *limbus,* meaning border or edge) because it forms a kind of border around the brain stem. Today the limbic lobe together with certain adjacent deep structures including the amygdala is known as the limbic system. Research suggests that specific affective functions (e.g., some emotions) are developed in this region—such as those which induce females to nurse and protect their toddlers and the playful moods that engender ludic behaviors. Emotions and feelings, like wrath, fright, passion, love, hate, joy, and sadness, which are mammalian inventions, originate in the limbic system.

It is important to stress that all the structures in the brain interconnect intensively. Some contribute more than others to this or that kind of emotion, but no one is by itself responsible for any specific emotional state. The prefrontal area is connected to the limbic region, so when it suffers a lesion, the person loses his or her sense of social responsibility (associated with the limbic system) as well as the capacity for concentration and abstraction (associated with the prefrontal area). When prefrontal lobotomy was used for treatment of certain psychiatric disturbances, the patients entered into a stage of "affective buffer," no longer showing any sign of joy, sadness, hope or despair. In their words or attitudes, no traces of affection could be detected.

Neuroscience, emotion, and values

What is the relationship between emotions, on the one hand, and values, on the other hand? I claim that emotions are connected to values because they involve appraisals. So, we can even suggest that emotions are correlates of values. The simplest version of this view is the claim that to feel one type of indignation (emotion) is to believe or judge that a situation is unjust—that is, if we believe a situation is unjust, we will become angry when confronted with it. In keeping with this view, one would see a correspondence between the importance a person ascribes to a value and the frequency of his or her emotional experiences related to that value. Therefore, we would expect to find the following:

- Fear associated with security values (People who frequently feel afraid in daily life ascribe great importance to security values because both fear and security values share the goal of realizing safety.)

- Feelings of disgust and contempt negatively related to conformity values

- Feelings of affection and concern for others related to the values of benevolence and universalism (Both express pro-social tendencies.)

- Feelings of pride related to achievement and self-direction values (Both express the importance of success and goal-attainment.)

- Feelings of guilt and shame related to conformity values (Whereas pride often involves a positive valuation of the self, shame and guilt involve negative self-evaluation, often following failures to live up to moral or social standards.)

Therefore, emotions are triggered by the brain following a sequence involving values. In the tri-axial model is an entire axis of emotional values. One of these that has been studied frequently is empathy. Empathy is a value that allows us to relate to the emotional states of others. This value is critical in regulating social interactions as it enables an individual to effect social bonding and exhibit care for others. Interestingly, scientists studying empathy in both children and animals have concluded that it is a major ingredient in explaining human and primate behavior. We see compelling evidence for the strength of the empathic reaction in scientists' findings that rhesus monkeys refuse to pull a chain that delivers food to them if doing so shocks a companion. These monkeys literally starve themselves to avoid inflicting pain on another.

Using values to manage emotions

Can you imagine a world with no emotions? No happiness, no sadness, no anxiety, no love, no pleasure, no pain, no frustration, no urges . . . no addiction. Every single one of us simply going about our day, doing whatever it is we are supposed to do (whatever that might be in a world without emotion). Don't just read this and move on. Take a few minutes to really imagine it. Imagine what your life would be like without emotions. Imagine what your soul would be like without emotions. Consider this, without getting too philosophical: Would you even have a soul? It *should* make you think.

Without emotions, you and I would be nothing more than physical bodies and the electrical impulses that produce the energy to run them. All thoughts would be functional. There would be no good or bad. No evil. No hatred. No love. In essence, we would be machines. What makes us human is our emotions. What allows us to experience the wonders of life—as well as the sorrow—is our emotions. Without emotions, not one of us would ever struggle with a single compulsive behavior. There would be no addiction. Life would be . . . *wonderful?* Now, take this one step further: If a life without emotions equals a life without certain behaviors, can controlling these behaviors can be reduced to the "simple" task of managing our emotions? When we learn to manage our emotions, we have learned to manage our behavior.

There are two types of emotions you need to be aware of in the addictive environment: value-based emotions and behavior-based emotions. Physiologically, they may be identical. Behavior-based emotions are the emotions that are experienced as a result of the triggering stimuli and the compulsive ritualistic behavior that follows. And so that we are clear, the "behavior" can be fantasy, masturbation, pursuing a romantic interest, stalking, smoking, drinking, gambling, eating, or any other action that has the ability to alter one's emotions (which can be just about any behavior imaginable—in the right circumstances). Such stimuli and behavior elicit immediate emotional reactions that can overwhelm a person's value system and over a sustained period, progressively destroy values altogether.

Value-based emotions are considerably different. They are based not on the reaction to stimuli, but in the preparation for it. They are based on a foundational commitment to long-term growth and life management. They are based in having developed an open and honest line of communication with oneself. Consider a marathon runner who sprints to the lead in the first couple hundred yards. The sprinting causes the runner to briefly experience the pleasure of winning, but the situation is not sustainable. Soon, his or her body will wear down, and all the tools that he could have used to win the race will no longer be useful. They will have lost their value. His entire race will be reduced to the single action of sprinting and resting . . . sprinting and resting. Addiction is similar. The behavior-based emotions are the sprint; the value-based emotions are the tools that will keep one in the race for the long haul.

Psychologists, therapists. and other health professionals normally work on altering and changing the negative consequences of behavioral-based emotions. In this book, I showed that by reducing incongruence or enhancing congruence of values, we can lead better lives both at work and off work. When our actions are consistent with our established values, positive emotions result. When our actions are based on spontaneous reaction, instability and chaos may result. The trick to managing the two in unison is being aware that behavior-based emotions can produce overwhelming changes in the here and now. Value-based emotions produce powerful, sustained emotions over time. There is a healthy time for both.

5.3 Values and spirituality: The inner voyage to coaching

Values, spirituality, and leadership effectiveness

Managers, professionals, and leaders often ask themselves, "Who am I?" and "What am I to do?" Decades ago, the reply to this question depended more on institutional and bureaucratic power, but now it depends on the capacity to articulate and inspire mutually selected values.[81] I mentioned earlier and want to reiterate that values were once considered by business leaders as "too soft" to be included in any serious approach to management, but they have now become a central part of organizational strategy. The concepts "Managing by Values" and "Coaching by Values," which I've introduced in this book are fast becoming the principal drivers for reengineering a sustainable, competitive, and emotional-spiritual

---

[81] For more, see: Ulrich, D., & Ulrich, W. (2010). *The Why of Work.* McGraw-Hill.

culture. A new form of transcendent spiritual leadership is arising from an internal philosophical commitment and is expressed in actions appealing to diverse cultural environments.[82]

The extent to which leaders are able to obtain sharing and consensus in the configuration of the tri-axial model is reflective of their leadership effectiveness. In the recent past, we have witnessed the downfall of leaders in almost every area—business, politics, religion, sports, and more. There might be thousands of reasons for these failures. But I believe that almost all of them are connected by one underlying thread—values. I have identified three principal reasons for these failures, all based on values:

- **The leaders lose sight of what is really important:** Many leaders distinguish themselves by their ability to "think big." But when their focus shifts, they suddenly start thinking small. They micromanage, they get caught up in details, and they become consumed with the trivial and unimportant. A more subtle leadership derailer is the obsession with doing rather than becoming. The good work of leadership is usually a result of who the leader is. What the leader does then flows naturally from inner vision and character. It is possible for a leader to become too action-oriented and, in the process, lose touch with the more important development of self.

- **The leader is engaged in an ethics slip:** A leader's credibility is the result of two aspects: what he or she does (competency) and who he or she is (character and personality). A discrepancy between these two creates an integrity problem. One of the highest principles of leadership is integrity. Ample research has shown that a respected leader is one keeps her promises. When integrity ceases to be a leader's top priority, when a compromise of ethics is rationalized away as necessary for the greater good,

---

[82]   For more, see: Dolan, S. L. (2010, December 10–11). *Coaching by values: The leadership spiritual connections.* Paper presented at the 1ˢᵗ Inaugural Conference on the Management of Spirituality, Vienna, Austria; Raich, M., Dolan S. L., & Eisler, R. (2010, February). Leveraging the corporate ecosystem and the new innovative role for human resource management. *Effective Executive, 12*(2), 30–34.

when achieving results becomes more important than the means to their achievement, a leader steps onto the stage of failure. Such a leader often sees followers as pawns, a mere means to an end, thus confusing manipulation with leadership. These leaders lose empathy. They cease to be people perceivers and become people pleasers, using popularity to ease the guilt of lapsed integrity.

- **The leader manifests lost touch or a loss of passion:** Leaders fail because they are moving away from their first love and dream. Paradoxically, the hard work of leadership should be fulfilling and even fun. But when leaders lose sight of the dream that compelled them to accept the responsibility of leadership, they can find themselves working for causes that mean little to them. They must stick to what they love, what motivated them originally, if they are to maintain the fulfillment of leadership.

Therefore, a new leadership framework is needed to enable leaders to understand the true drivers of leadership. The model needs to enable them to stay on track by following their love, passion, and compassion. They need to find the balance between their instrumental values and spiritual values; they need to find the answer to three basic questions: Why did I initially assume leadership? Have those reasons changed? Do I still want to lead?

The tri-axial model of values for alignment and realignment has been proposed as the framework for explaining excellence in various fields. In the 2010 world football cup in South Africa, some national teams ended in disaster because of their failure to share values, especially between the leader (the coach) and the followers (the players). In the case of the French team, we can see the incongruence between the coach's values and those of the players. By contrast, excellence (as seen in the Spanish team) can be explained by the degree of harmony and shared values (e.g., competitiveness, hard work, team spirit, collegiality) among team members and leadership. Business leaders should take a note from these experiences in the sports world. Technical competencies alone do not generate success. It requires collective passion and team synergy. The task of an effective leader in the twenty-first century is to build a culture that aligns these values with the corporate core (key organizational values), creating corporate well-being.

Corporate well-being is achieved when the core values of an organization are shared and aligned with the mission and vision of the organization.

The missing link: The spiritual values of an inspired leader

Avinash Kaushik identifies three "spires" of great leadership: Aspire, Perspire, Inspire:[83]

- **Aspire:** To have a great ambition or ultimate goal; to strive toward an end. Great leaders aspire for greatness—for themselves, for their teams, for their companies, for every individual around them. They are not content with what exists or what is possible. They are long-term thinkers. They have an elevator pitch handy that articulates what their vision is, what they are trying to get done, and how the team they lead can contribute to value for the employees, the customers, and the shareholders. Great leaders are hungry; they want more and are never satisfied with status quo. They want to change the world (even if the "world" is their little ecosystem) for the benefit of their employees, their companies, and themselves (in that order). An exemplar of such a leadership is the late Akio Morita, the cofounder and chairman of Sony, who was known for the clarity with which he viewed his role as the company's leader: *"My most important mission is to create a company where I can satisfy the people who work there, then come the clients, and only after come the shareholders."*

- **Perspire:** To work hard, to be industrious, and to sweat. It also means to resist pressures, to perform with great diligence or energy, and to sustain effort. Great leaders work harder and smarter with every passing day. Great leaders are not necessarily the slave drivers who stay at work until midnight or make people work weekends (which can become stressful and counterproductive[84]); great

---

83   Kaushik, A. (2006). Three "Spires" of Great Leadership. http://www.kaushik. net/avinash/2006/08/three-spires-of-great-leadership.html.

84   For more on this, see: Moodie, S., Dolan, S. L., & Arsenault, A. (2011, February 24–27). *Exploring the multiple linkages between metabolic syndrome and stress: An empirical analysis of the relationships between stress, health, and metabolic*

leaders simply bring 110% of themselves to work during work hours and set an awesome example for all those around them. Great leaders stay focused, and they don't give up easily. Because of their passion for creating meaning, they are able to get each person around them to bring his or her complete self to work. An exemplary model of such a great leader was John D. Rockefeller, who used to say: "*Get up early, work hard, strike oil.*"

- **Inspire:** To affect, guide, or fill with enlivening or exalting emotion; to stimulate to action. Great leaders' magnificent success (personal and professional) comes from their ability to inspire those around them to contribute to the creation of meaning in this world. Exemplary figures of this type of leader are Nelson Mandela and the late Martin Luther King, who kept their dreams and inspirations intact through years of hardship and in the face of imprisonment, hatred, and all manner of injustices.

Kaushik considers "inspire" to be an essential element of a great leader. Looking at his definition and taking it a bit further, can we define an inspirational leader? There are many different ways to view the term *inspirational*, because it means different things to different people. The English *inspire* is derived from the Latin verb *inspirare*: "to breathe into," "breathe upon," or "breathe in." In one of its first uses in English, a use that is now archaic, it literally meant "to infuse with life by breathing." Even though that particular use is now archaic, it has certainly influenced the evolution of the word in all its forms (*inspirational, inspired,* and so on), so we could say that when a person inspires others, he or she breathes in (finds inspiration) and then breathes into (others).

An inspirational leader breathes into others and makes them feel alive, and they, in turn, want to follow. But before inspiring others, a leader must be inspired; he or she must first breathe in inspiration. I think this is the closest I can come to defining spirituality in the context of leadership. Inspiration is personal and specific to each leader. Where one leader will find inspiration, another may not. Some may find inspiration inside themselves, others may find it in the external world, and many leaders

---

syndrome among Catalan nurses. Paper presented at International Conference on Prehypertension & Cardio-Metabolic Syndrome, Vienna, Austria.

will find it in both places. But all are inspired and all have the ability to engender that inspiration in others.

Internal inspiration emerges from dealing with the most essential aspects of being: What is my core purpose in life? What am I passionate about? What is it, within me, that inspires me to take action? How will I follow and express that inspiration? *External* inspiration emerges from contacts with the external world: Who inspires me? What are the characteristics of the people or things that inspire me? What is it in the external world that inspires me to action?

The most distinguishing characteristic of visionary, effective leaders is their relentless insistence on sticking to their personal values. Visionary leadership is based on a balanced expression of the spiritual, mental, emotional, and physical dimensions. It requires core values, clear vision, empowering relationships, and innovative action. When one or more of these dimensions are missing, leadership cannot manifest a vision.

A commitment to values is an outstanding characteristic of all visionary leaders. They embody a sense of personal integrity and radiate a sense of energy, vitality, and will. Will is standing in a spiritual state of being. Will is a spiritual attribute, which allows a leader to stand for something. Because we have already dealt with ethical, emotional, and economic values (in the tri-axial model), in this section, we will explore the connection of visionary leadership to spiritual values.

The category "spiritual values" does not comprise entirely new values. Some of the values in this set might traditionally be considered emotional values or ethical values. The primary reason for differentiating them is that spiritual values come from a beyond-body perspective of life and universe.[85] The emotional values dimension focuses more on the feelings, attitudes, and traits in individuals: the spiritual values dimension focus on another level of the individuals, where they create the significance of their being. Unlike other values, spiritual values need not always have the characteristics of direct instrumentality. Spirituality is notoriously hard

---

[85] For more on this, see: Garcia-Zamor, J. C. (2003). Workplace spirituality and organizational performance. *Public Administration Review, 63*(3), 355–364; Coetzer, G., Biberman, J., & Tischler, L. (2008). Transcending belief: A non-theistic model for operationalizing spiritual values, practices and states, and their relationship to workplace behavior. *Interbeing, 2*(1), 19–30; Veer, P. van der. (2009). Spirituality in modern society. *Social Research, 76*(4), 1097–1120.

to define. Giacalone and Jurkiewicz, for example, provide 14 different definitions of spirituality. A sample includes the following:[86]

- A personal life principle that animates a transcendent quality of relationship with God

- The human striving for the transforming power present in life; the attraction and movement of the human person toward the divine

- The personal expression of ultimate concern

- A transcendent dimension within human experience

Others describe spirituality according to various characteristics, ranging from the personal to the supreme to interconnectedness to a guiding plan for our lives. In sum, there is no universally accepted definition of spirituality.

Perhaps in the future, the tri-axial model of culture will be converted into a quad-axial model, with the new spiritual dimension providing a place for one to register such values as life purpose, virtue, unity, truth, and hope.

Leadership effectiveness, spiritual values, and the paths to happiness

In order to better understand the connection between leadership effectiveness, spirituality, and happiness in relation to the world of work, we need to understand the concept of visionary leadership, which is often equated with the ability to see higher spiritual forces at work behind the scenes of events. Many visionary leaders seek alignment with these supporting and redemptive forces. Both George Washington and Winston Churchill spoke about the help they received from a "guiding hand." Churchill said, "We have a guardian because we serve a great cause, and we shall have that guardian as long as we serve that cause faithfully." Sojourner Truth, a former slave, was guided by an inner spiritual experience to preach the emancipation of slaves and women's rights all over the country

---

[86] Giacalone, R. A., & Jurkiewicz, C. L. (2003). Toward a science of workplace spirituality. In *Handbook of Workplace Spirituality and Organizational Performance*. M. E. Sharpe.

during the U.S. Civil War. President Anwar Sadat of Egypt had a vision in which Mohammed told him to create peace in the Middle East. This is the hidden story behind the Camp David Accords. Even Albert Einstein, who considered himself to be nonreligious, turned to the divine and to spirituality, which he saw as complementary to science. Einstein spoke of a "spirit manifest in the laws of the universe" and his sincere belief in a "God who reveals Himself in the harmony of all that exists."

Here are some famous quotes about visionary spiritual business leaders:

> The companies that survive longest are the ones that work out what they uniquely can give to the world—not just growth or money, but their excellence, their respect for others, or their ability to make people happy. Some call those things a soul.
>
> —Charles Handy

> A leader has the vision and conviction that a dream can be achieved. He inspires the power and energy to get it done.
>
> —Ralph Lauren

> A leader's role is to raise people's aspirations for what they can become and to release their energies so they will try to get there.
>
> —David Gergen

Visionary leaders understand that spirit at work is all about finding meaning and purpose, beyond self, through work. It involves profound feelings of well-being, a belief that one's work makes a contribution, a sense of connection to others, and a feeling of common purpose.

Visionary leadership is much more than directing others. It starts from within: from seeing problems to seeing possibilities, from seeing the glass half empty to seeing the glass half full, and from looking outside for answers to finding them within. Leading from within is a shift to focusing on inner knowing and inner strengths. Even if a visionary leader's original inspiration arose from something in the outside world (the "external inspiration" I discussed above), that external phenomenon effected an internal transformation within the leader. The key to understanding this is values.

Times of crisis and times of enlightenment are times with potential for change and growth. In these times, people often begin to question their values, priorities, and ways of living and working. Significant and painful life events, including the death of a loved one, the break-up of one's family, illness, organizational downsizing, or loss of job can be viewed as opportunities as well as challenges. Sometimes referred to as the "dark night of the soul," these events tend to bring forth the need to create meaning. And the meaning we ascribe to them is central to how we emerge on the other side. Profound spiritual experiences such as near-death experiences or personal epiphany experiences that occur while in a sacred place or being in nature can be similarly transformative.

Visionary leaders who aspire and inspire understand that to engender meaning in themselves and in their followers, they need to show them paths to happiness. Based on growing trends in positive psychology, Seligman proposed three paths to happiness: the life of pleasure, the life of engagement, and the life of meaning.[87] The "pleasurable life" is what we experience when we participate in enjoyable activities like playing games with our children, sharing a good meal, or taking holidays. The "life of engagement" is being wholly involved in, thoroughly understanding, and using our strengths in any activity that we find challenging and rewarding—work, play, or family life, among others. When we experience this deep engagement and total absorption, we are said to be in a state of flow,[88] a state that we discussed briefly in chapter 3. Finally, a "life of meaning" develops when an individual uses his or her strengths for the purpose of something larger than self. A "meaningful life" comes from serving others and may include attending to the family, caring for other people, volunteer activities, or work. The visionary and inspirational leader can help followers move from the life of pleasure to the life of meaning.

A study that reviewed more than 150 research results shows a clear consistency between spiritual values and practices and effective

---

[87] Seligman, M. E. P. (2008, July). Positive health [Issue supplement]. *Applied Psychology, 57*, 3–18.

[88] Gardner, H., Csikszentmihalyi, M., & Damon, W. (2002). *Good Business: Leadership, Flow, and the Making of Meaning.* Basic Books.

leadership.[89] Values that have long been considered spiritual ideals, such as integrity, honesty, and humility, have been demonstrated to have an effect on leadership success. Practices traditionally associated with spirituality have also been shown to be connected to leadership effectiveness. All of the following practices have been emphasized in spiritual teachings, and they have also been found to be critical leadership skills: showing respect for others, demonstrating fair treatment, expressing caring and concern, listening responsively, recognizing the contributions of others, and engaging in reflective practice.

Workplace spirituality can be used as a framework of organizational values that promote employees' experience of transcendence through the work process and facilitate their sense of being connected in a way that provides feelings of compassion and joy. Spiritual values do not demonstrate a direct instrumentality like the tri-axial values, but demonstrate a significant indirect instrumentality by creating a platform on which the other values may be aligned. (If this seems to contradict what I said in the previous section about the future of the tri-axial model and the quad-axial model, read on. I will discuss this in the next section.) Many leadership theories emphasize the need for the leader to articulate an inspiring vision, but as I've emphasized throughout this book, what is most important is not the words but the actions that follow.

Toward a new, universal values–based leadership model

I argue that leaders in the twenty-first century will need to have the capacity to strike a balance between all four sets of values: **economic-pragmatic, ethical-social, emotional-developmental,** and **spiritual.** I refer to such leaders as "universal" leaders. From our previous discussions, both here and throughout the book, some values suggest themselves as candidates for the proposed fourth axis: cooperation and partnership; appreciation of diversity; respect for life; respect for nature and ecosystems; and a meaningful work and life for the majority of the people in an organization.

The universal values–based leader undertakes the role of identifying and promoting the values—from all dimensions, or axes—shared by the

---

[89] Reave, L. (2005). Spiritual values and practices related to leadership effectiveness. *The Leadership Quarterly, 16*(5), 655–687.

stakeholders of the organization. This leader should aspire to become a leader, perspire to achieve goals, and inspire himself or herself to raise the bar for the spiritual contents. The model for this new kind of leader is presented schematically in exhibit 5.1

Exhibit 5.1: A universal values–based leader

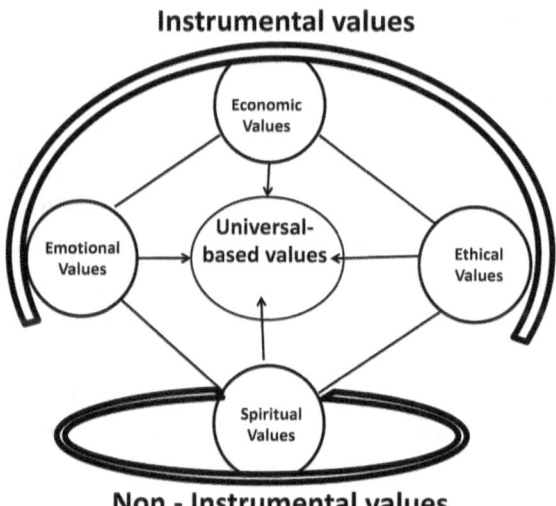

SOURCE: Adapted from Raich, M., & Dolan, S. L. (2008). *Beyond,* p. 119. Palgrave Macmillan. Used with authors' permission.

Leaders who practice this type of leadership will increase organizational well-being. Notice that I say organizational *well-being* rather than organizational *performance.* The three dimensions of values in the tri-axial model can be instrumental in enhancing performance or profits as long as they do not deter from the quality of life and meaning of work. The spiritual values axis, however, should contain non-instrumental properties and need not necessarily be directly linked to organizational performance. This is in accordance with the fundamental paradox of organizational spirituality articulated by Lips-Wiersrma: "Those who practice spirituality in order to achieve better corporate results undermine both its practice and its ultimate benefits."[90]

For use in evaluating leadership and guiding leaders, I propose adding another axis to the model, the axis of spirituality, thus creating a "quad-axial" model. True leadership requires values from all four axes, or dimensions. The four axes, however, like the three axes of the 3Es tri-axial model, need not be symmetrical.

A spiritually friendly workplace respects people's deepest values and belief systems and allows them to incorporate these values in their daily work interactions, bringing meaning to work. At first, some people may feel uneasy about using words such as *spirituality* and *spiritual* when discussing workplace values, but this is often because they are confusing spirituality with religion. Spirituality does not imply adherence to a religion nor is it defined by an explicit set of religious beliefs or practices. On the contrary, some people are religious without being spiritual, while others are spiritual without being religious. Spirituality is an individual contract that one makes with oneself; it may involve religion, but it doesn't need to. It is a contract about beliefs—often involving a transcendent other, but not always; it may be based on nature, the universe and its direction (e.g., teleology), or even physics, but it *always* involves how we see and value other human beings and the world. It is how people identify themselves to the outside world, how they view the world, how they interact with others, and on what fundamental basis they make decisions.

Talking about spiritualism and leadership is risky business. Leaders are normally judged by hard numbers, the added value they might bring or have brought to wealth creation.[91] The "experiencing of life," an existential agenda, is often missing from the pages of management journals. No matter how broad the range of perceptions of spirituality may be, all definitions in one way or another involve ideas expressed by the word *interconnectedness*. In my experience, the Coaching by Values framework

---

90 Lips-Wiersrma, M. (2007, June). *Practical compassion: Toward a critical spiritual foundation for corporate responsibility.* Paper presented at the Academy of Management meeting.

91 Hess and Cameron have written an extraordinary book arguing that leading by values, including spiritual values, can convert organizations into high-performing organizations. See: Hess, E. D., & Cameron, K. S. (2006). *Leading with Values.* Cambridge University Press.

can serve as the link between the instrumental values of the real business world and the spiritual need for experiencing life. Some people call this combination of the body (materialistic drivers) and the soul (spiritual needs) "spiritual intelligence."

Leadership in the twenty-first century needs to go beyond pure pragmatism to encompass a more holistic perception of the world. Coaching by Values using the four-axis (quad-axial) model can be a benchmark for assessing and understanding a deeper meaning of life. Clearly not all leaders can be described as spiritual leaders, just as not all leaders can act as coaches, but as we enter the Third Millennium, thousands of individuals representing a new breed of visionary leaders in all fields of human endeavor are emerging around the world. They are leading a quiet revolution energized by the power of the soul. Perhaps by embracing and supporting those who lead from their core spiritual values, we can deepen those leadership qualities in ourselves.

As A. Deshpande and S. Shukla have said, "We are all spiritual beings. Unleashing the whole capability of the individual—mind, body, and spirit—gives enormous power to the organization. Spirituality unlocks the real sense of significance of the organization's purpose."[92]

---

[92]   Deshpande, A., & Shukla, S. (2010, August 11–13). Spirituality at workplace. *Proceedings of the AIMS International Conference on Value-Based Management*, p. 848.

CBV Reflection ♣ ♠ ♥

How Spiritual Are You? A Short Quiz*

To find out how spiritual you are, take this test, which is adapted from a personality inventory devised by Washington University psychiatrist Robert C. Cloninger, author of *Feeling Good: The Science of Well-Being*

1. I often feel so connected to the people around me that it is like there is no separation between us.   True   False

2. I often do things to help protect animals and plants from extinction.   True   False

3. I am fascinated by the many things in life that cannot be scientifically explained.   True   False

4. Often I have unexpected flashes of insight or understanding while relaxing.   True   False

5. I sometimes feel so connected to nature that everything seems to be part of one living organism.   True   False

6. I seem to have a "sixth sense" that sometimes allows me to know what is going to happen.   True   False

7. Sometimes I have felt like I was part of something with no limits or boundaries in time and space.   True   False

8. I am often called "absent-minded" because I get so wrapped up in what I am doing that I lose track of everything else.   True   False

9. I often feel a strong sense of unity with all the things around me.   True   False

10. Even after thinking about something a long time, I have learned to trust my feelings more than my logical reasons.   True   False

11. I often feel a strong spiritual or emotional connection with all the people around me.   True   False

12. Often when I am concentrating on something, I lose awareness of the passage of time.   True   False

13. I have made real personal sacrifices in order to make the world a better place, like trying to prevent war, poverty, and injustice.   True   False

14. I have had experiences that made my role in life so clear to me that I felt very happy and excited.   True   False

15. I believe that I have experienced extrasensory perception.   True   False

16. I have had moments of great joy in which I suddenly had a clear, deep feeling of oneness with all that exists.   True   False

17. Often when I look at an ordinary thing, something wonderful happens. I get the feeling that I am seeing it fresh for the first time.   True   False

18. I love the blooming of flowers in the spring as much as seeing an old friend again.   True   False

19. It often seems to other people like I am in another world because I am so completely unaware of things going on around me.   True   False

20. I believe that miracles happen.   True   False

> **SCORING:** Give yourself one point for each True and no points for each False.
>
> 14–20 points means you are a highly spiritual person, a real mystic
> 12–13 points means that you have spiritual awareness, that you are easily lost in the moment
> 8–11 points means that you scored average on the spirituality scale; there is a room for further spirituality development if you desire to follow this path
> 6–7 points means that you are a practical, empirical person, lacking self–transcendence
> 1–5 points means that you are highly skeptical, resistant to developing spiritual awareness

* **NOTE:** This is a quick-and-dirty test. It is designed to give you a *general* idea about your level of spirituality. **SOURCE:** © *Robert C. Cloninger, Sansone Family Center for Well-being, Washington University, St. Louis, Mo.* Used with author's permission.

5.4 Values in the New Age (new global needs and new paradigms)

Our universe is changing as I write. And it is about to change even more. We are witnessing the birth of global values. A host of nations in the Middle East are transforming as the masses discover the values of democracy and freedom and struggle to break from tyrannical rule (e.g., Egypt, Tunisia, and Libya, to name a few). These events were predictable, but no one knew exactly when they would occur.

In 2008, I coauthored a futuristic book, *Beyond*, with Mario Raich in which we argued that there is an urgent need for humanity to leave its comfort zone before it becomes too late.[93] The world of tomorrow will be very different from the world of today, or the world of yesterday. But in what ways will it be different? What will that world look like? It is up to us.

---

[93] See: Raich, M., & Dolan, S. L. (2008). *Beyond: Business and Society in Transformation.* London: Palgrave Macmillan.

In *Beyond*, we defined six key areas in which dramatic shifts in basic values are needed immediately if we are to ensure the survival of our species: society, religion, environment, science and technology, business, and politics. We drew a roadmap to the future and explored the ways in which previously unimaginable changes and developments will and are transforming the social and business landscape of the twenty-first century.

In the new world, the actions of business leaders may well be judged in regard to their compliance with universal human values, eco-friendliness, and meaningfulness. Today, we can see customers requesting, and we envision down the road legislators demanding, eco-friendliness. The millions of eco-minded organizations could create a powerful alliance of people caring for the future. The spike in people searching for meaningfulness on the job is an indication that a significant percentage of the population is already look beyond the greed-based economism that has dominated the Western world since the last quarter of the past century.

As we look toward the future, we must also look to indigenous peoples. They have been able to survive longer than any other existing civilizations, in part because of their appreciation for the natural world. They recognize the Earth as a partner whose resources are precious gifts not to be taken for granted and depleted. Their experiences mastering crises that threatened their existence and their appreciation of the systemic connections among all living things have much to teach us. This interconnectedness requires empathy. Scientific research suggests that empathy is the foundation of morality, and many aspects of morality appear to be hard-wired in the brain. In addition, emotions are central to moral thinking. The appreciation that we live in an interconnected system comprising all we can see, hear, and feel requires—and in turn generates—empathy. Indigenous cultures and the stories they tell are an invaluable source of insights.

Exhibit 5.2: Embedded emergent values: A holistic view

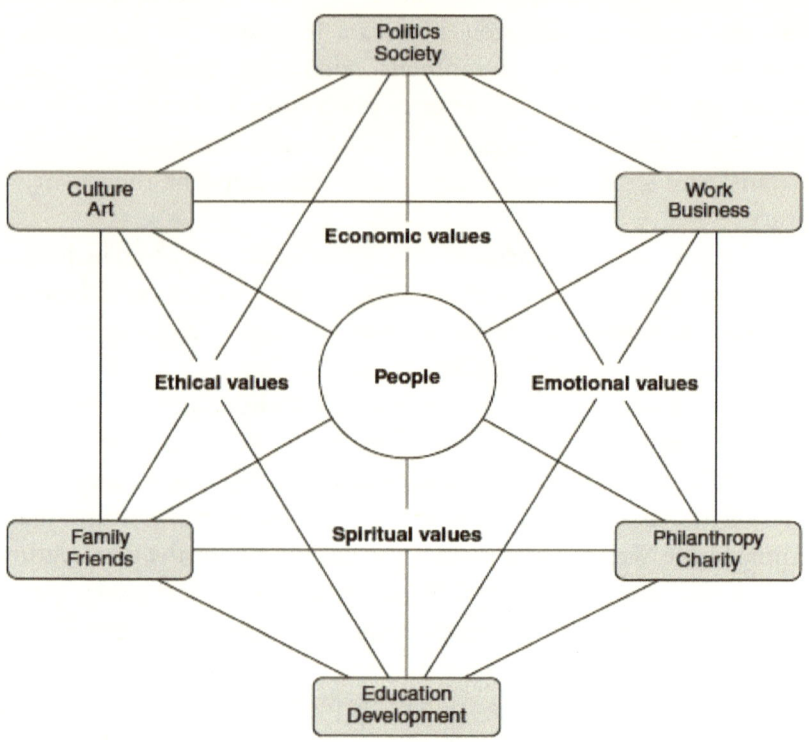

SOURCE: Raich, M., & Dolan, S. L. (2008). *Beyond,* p. 89. Palgrave Macmillan. Used with authors' permission.

Exhibit 5.2 represents a holistic view of people's values and attitudes, which change as a function of changes that occur in the immediate environment, which in this global century may encompass the entire planet. As it shows, PEOPLE (us) are sitting in the center surrounded by a several boxes that represent the elements of our environment. At the top of the figure are POLITICS and SOCIETY; in the upper-right-hand is the way we WORK and the way do BUSINESS. All of these—and all of us—are profoundly influenced by CULTURE and the ARTS, by FAMILY and FRIENDS. At the base of the figure are the EDUCATION and DEVELOPMENT opportunities open to us. These are one of the most significant determinants of a person's success (or not) and well-being (or lack of it). Finally, the social safety net—whether it is provided by Social Security or by PHILANTHROPY and CHARITY—is a guarantor of survival if everything else has gone wrong.

As this figure shows us, nothing less than models that are systemic and holistic will get us from here to a sustainable future. We need models with which we can co-create holistic and systemic scenarios of the future that encompass all the elements of our environment and take into account all four dimensions of values. We need to expand our concept of value-based *management* by embracing the value-based *organization*. We must recognize and appreciate the impact of values on any organization, any system, any culture, and we must craft value-creation models and models for determining the impacts of specific values.

The movement to identify and promote the values shared by societies around the world is relatively new but burgeoning, with several initiatives and projects doing just that. The most important is probably the Earth Charter Initiative, with formal endorsements by more than 2,000 organizations including national and international bodies such as UNESCO (United Nations Educational, Social and Cultural Organization). Its declaration of principles for a just, sustainable, and peaceful world is a call for the shared responsibility of all humanity. It was created during a ten-year grassroots process with input from thousands of people in many countries around the world. This widely recognized, global consensus statement on ethics and values for a sustainable future is based on 16 principles organized into four major categories:

- respect and care for the community of life
- ecological integrity
- social and economic justice
- democracy, nonviolence, and peace

This is a step toward filling an urgent need to identify the shared code of ethics and conduct underlying all human societies, defining universal human values, and formalizing them in a global compact.

The creative and spiritual society[94]

With the right values, a creative society can generate real solutions to the existential key issues facing humanity and our planet. At the

---

[94] This section is based on a message Mario Raich and I delivered in a recent paper: Raich, M., & Dolan, S. L. (2009). Managing in the new landscape.

beginning of chapter 4, I used the metaphor of a compass to describe an individual's values. Now imagine that compass providing direction for an entire society—and for each of its members. Keeping our eye on it, and using it to find the direction again if we start to lose our way, we will be free to imagine and implement solutions at the farthest reaches of the mind. With the support of artificial intelligence entities, we will be able to develop the full potential of our creativity. Virtual reality already gives us the space to explore proposed solutions and test their impact on humanity in ways we never could have foreseen. New and more powerful methods of crafting and testing creative solutions will be developed. But we need to move from searching to finding and from finding to implementing creative solutions.

The first step toward the development of a creative society is overcoming the "gender issue," which has grown into a gender creativity gap. At a time when we need every iota of intellectual and spiritual creativity, we are (willfully at times) ignoring a huge reservoir of it—the "feminine," which resides in every female and to some extent, in every male. The dominance of reason ("masculine") has come at the expense of intuition and emotional intelligence ("feminine"). The feminine way of thinking, being, and doing is crucial for true partnership and care; it is an essential energizer for the imagination. The demonization of the feminine—and its flip side, the worship of a crabbed and caricatured version of the feminine from afar—has driven the polarization of the masculine and the feminine through the whole population and civilization diminishing not only women but also males with feminine abilities, thus diminishing the entire society.

The resolution of the gender issue requires going much deeper and further than creating gender equality in the workplace, the polling place, and the like. In this regard, we should consider very seriously the framework that Riane Eisler has been developing and her suggestions for its implementation. She has been doing remarkable work over the past 20 years or so through her international Center for Partnership Studies (see Riane Eisler vignette in this section and my discussion of her ideas in chapter 2).

In any discussion of developing solutions to the challenges confronting humanity, we should take a moment to consider the concept "innovation." Innovation by its very nature has a lasting impact on the environment.

Effective Executive, 12(10), 48-56.

It has led to wonderful advances, but it is a transformative change that disrupts systems and may endanger that which gives our lives value. Some innovations in medicine have saved entire segments of societies around the globe from death. But innovations for the sake of profit in the short term may cause products to be rushed to the market before their effects (on humans or nature) are understood or known. Innovations in farming led to the Dust Bowl in the United States in the 1930s, destroying some of the North American continent's most fertile land.

Depending on the context (and whether one's vision is short-term or long-term), an innovation may be perceived as a negative or positive. Over the long term, an innovation will show whether it in fact represented value creation or value destruction. The value of innovation is contextual in that it depends on what one values. For example, cutting a tree is a transformation, because it is irreversible, but it is a destructive change. Clear-cutting rain forests or old growth forests are large-scale examples of this. In the hands of a carpenter, however, a single felled tree may be the starting point for the creation of something that brings value to people—a chair, an armoire, or a bed. So where do we draw the line between "ethical" and "unethical" innovation?

Capitalism drives unethical innovation. In its rabid search for markets and its need for ever-greater accumulation of capital, it is transforming nature (our ecosystems) and has already resulted in the extinction of some species. It is highly volatile; it goes wherever it encounters the most favorable conditions for itself (safety, security, stability, low taxes, growth potential, and so on) with no regard for the quality of human life or the sanctity of nature, turning all human abilities and natural resources into numbers, churning them up and spitting them out.

All evidence points to the need to go beyond capitalism. If we don't, it will destroy itself—and probably us along with it. Taming, reforming, and reinventing capitalism are not options. It has shown itself to be a wild beast that behaves only behind the bars of a strong authoritarian governmental cage, and even then only for so long. When freed, it devours everything, transforming it into capital, reifying the imagination, turning all of the earth's gifts into products never to be regained, and leaving behind it a wake of death.

Capitalism also damages the mental health of the people who support it. Sound mental health is a universal goal of any human activity, and capitalism is rendering it unattainable.

The following are some of the key aspects of the capitalist system that corrode sound mental health:

- greed—for power, position, prestige, and money
- envy—regarding others' achievements, success, rewards
- egotism—about one's own accomplishments
- suspicion, anger, frustration, and paranoia
- anguish—over constant comparisons

We need a new direction for human society. We desperately need alternatives to which we can aspire and which will provide us with new meaning. At the societal and the corporate levels, we need to envision the future and venture into it. We must immediately develop initiatives to create social values and cease activities that forestall the opportunities of future generations. As employees, we can help an organization take society and the future into account. As individuals, we can help the global community through local action. And in everything we do, we can focus on the future. This is the only sure way to avoid unwanted surprises.

We need to strengthen partnership values and leave behind the old programming of conquest and control that has kept us from balanced and harmonious relations with ourselves, with others, and with nature.

A Dramatic Global Shift from Domination to Partnership and Care Is Needed "Yesterday"

Riane Eisler

People all over the world are questioning matters that only a few generations ago were generally seen as "just the way things are." We are living in a world of transformation. We have witnessed the demise of the communist-socialist economic system. And it looks like the capitalistic Western economy as we know it is in real crisis, with some saying it has already collapsed. Hand in hand with these economic upheavals are social upheavals as more and more people are reexamining their values.

In my early writings (e.g., *The Chalice and the Blade: Our History, Our Future*), I showed that cultural values are inextricably interconnected

---

with what is considered normal regarding the roles and relations of women and men. In other words, what is considered "masculine" or "feminine" and their relative valuation profoundly affect cultural and economic systems. Using historical and evolutionary analyses, I showed the danger to our world of the subordination of half of humanity and the values stereotypically associated with that half. I argued—and continue to argue--that allowing the stereotypical roles and relations of women and men to persist will lead to disaster.

I want to emphasize that the problem is not men. It is the way male identity has been defined in what I call "domination systems" (man over man, man over woman, race over race, man over nature, and so on), where "masculinity" is equated with domination and conquest—of women, other men, nature.

The real alternative to a patriarchal, or male-dominant, society is not a matriarchy but a society based on a very different way of organizing social relations: the partnership model. In this model, beginning with the most fundamental difference in our species—the difference between male and female—diversity is not equated with inferiority or superiority, dominating or being dominated. In systems oriented to this model, great value is given to stereotypically feminine values, such as caring and nonviolence, in men as well as women and in business and social policy. And rather than hierarchies of domination, where accountability and respect flow only from the bottom up, in partnership systems we find hierarchies of actualization, where power is used to empower rather than disempower others—whether by parents in families, teachers in schools, managers in businesses, or leaders in nations.

It is, therefore, not coincidental that our time—when the combination of high technology and a domination system of social organization poses a danger to all life on this earth—is a time when women and men all over the world are challenging stereotypical gender roles and relations. Nor is it coincidental that on the grassroots level, groups working for equality, development, and peace are proliferating—even against strong dominator resistance and intermittent regressions.

In a more recent book, *The Real Wealth of Nations*, I documented the real market costs of economic structures that are basically temples of worship in support of patriarchal and warrior cultures. These cultures often take for granted the so-called feminine soft values of peace-making, nurturing, educating, and creativity; they do not value them with real financial support. We can determine what a society cares about simply by looking at its expenditures. This sounds simplistic, but it's true. A society's values are embodied in its budget. For example, many countries in the world have huge military budgets, but their schools are falling apart. What does that tell us about what these societies value?

Rigid domination-based cultures (e.g., the Nazis or the Taliban) idealize the "traditional family," which is code for an authoritarian, highly punitive family in which males dominate women and children. This kind of family structure is foundational to societies that also idealize war, bloodshed, and destruction—domination and violence.

Perhaps we will accept, once and for all, that if we really value such things as caring and nonviolence, we must look at the roots of the values we have inherited. When we do this, we will be on our way to abandoning the domination paradigm, which at our level of technological development could take us to an evolutionary dead end.

Only then can we develop an economic system that is adaptive and supports the kind of values we want for ourselves and for our children. Our time of danger and upheaval offers us the opportunity to recognize that the real wealth of nations consists of the contributions of people and nature and to acknowledge that we need what we have not had: economic indicators, policies, and practices that give visibility and value to the most important human work: the work of caring for people, beginning in childhood, and for nature. We need a caring economics.

As Einstein said, the same thinking that created our problems can't solve them. Our children and the children of our children are looking beyond conventional categories such as capitalist vs. socialist, East vs. West, religious vs. secular, and technologically developed vs. undeveloped. They see that we need new categories that tell us what kinds of cultures support peace, creativity, and caring rather than violence, destructiveness, and insensitivity. They understand that we need new thinking.

When domination is accepted as a norm, certain values are dominant: authoritarianism (in the family and in society at large), the subordination of women and the feminine (whether in women or men), rigid hierarchies of domination in economics and society, and built-in violence. As we move toward the partnership side of the spectrum, we see more focus on values such as democracy, equality, and nonviolence.

But to realize, or make real, these values, we have to go deeper. We humans live by stories. Unfortunately many of the stories we inherited from earlier times teach that dominating or being dominated are the only alternatives. Stories offering a partnership alternative of relations built on mutual benefit, mutual respect, and mutual accountability are signs that a major revolution in consciousness is taking place. As are conversations in which we talk of power as empowering rather than disempowering and the many instances in which we can see that more and more people worldwide are no longer devaluing women and the feminine.

The emergence in bits and pieces of the belief that a partnership way of structuring human society is a viable possibility has enormous implications for both spirituality and morality. Spirituality becomes no longer an escape to otherworldly realms from the suffering inherent in a dominator world, but an active engagement in creating a better world right here on Earth. And rather than being used to coerce and dominate, morality is imbued with caring and love.

We can all play an active part in this transformation of economics, values, and societies. Indeed, we must, if we are to construct solid foundations for a more peaceful and sustainable future.

Riane Eisler is internationally known for her bestseller *The Chalice and the Blade*, now in 23 foreign editions, and *The Real Wealth of Nations: Creating a Caring Economics*, hailed by Archbishop Desmond Tutu as "a template for the better world we have been so urgently seeking." Dr. Eisler keynotes conferences worldwide, has been a pioneer in promoting peace and human rights, and has received many honors, including honorary PhD degrees. She teaches at the California Institute of Integral Studies (CIIS), is the author of more than 500 articles and book chapters based on her research, and is president of the Center for Partnership Studies, www.partnershipway.org, which promotes research, education, and advocacy toward building a more sustainable and equitable world. She can be contacted at center@partnershipway.org. For more information on Eisler and her work, go to http://www.rianeeisler.com/influence.html.

Conclusion

Human beings are endowed with spiritual capacities. Sages, philosophers, poets and artists, the founders of all the world's religions, and other thinkers, explorers, and seekers have shown this throughout history. An understanding of the positive virtues and values that reside in the spiritual gives individuals and societies the moral accountability that is the basis of human integrity. But even though values clarification is essential, so too is values education. This goes a step beyond critical analysis and intellectual appreciation and moves values into the realm of volition, stimulating the desire for improvement in ourselves, our families, our communities, and the world. Knowledge is impotent if not realized in action. We must translate our most precious principles and deeply held ideals into behaviors, individually and collectively.

The children of today will be the leaders of tomorrow. If they are to hold and embody the values and the awareness that will transition our world to a healthy future, we need to demonstrate these ourselves through our behaviors and give voice to them with our words. This is a task for parents, for educators, for managers, and for politicians.

We live in a world that is every day more interconnected and more interdependent, and there is no place to escape. Universal values are more acutely needed in this age of globalization than ever before. Every society needs to be bound together by common values so its members know what to expect of each other and are equipped with shared principles for managing their differences nonviolently, respectfully, and imaginatively. This is true across all cultures, from the smallest tribal body to the largest nation. And now, as our lives are affected almost instantly by things that people say and do on the far side of the world, it is increasingly true for us as a global community.

We must have global values in action that bind us together. In the end, history will judge us not by what we say but by what we do. Those who preach certain values loudest—values such as freedom, ethics, and morality, the rule of law and equality before the law—have a special obligation to live by those values in their own lives and their own societies, and to apply them to those they consider their enemies as well as their friends.

CBV Reflection ♣ ♠ ♥

Think of the key message(s) you retained after reading this chapter. Then complete the following sentences:

The principal points I liked in this chapter include

1._____

2._____

3._____

The principal points that I did not like or disagreed with in this chapter include

1._____

2._____

3._____

Appendices

- **Appendix 1**: Pool of Generic Values
- **Appendix 2:** Blank Template of the 3Es Tri-axial Model
- **Appendix 3:** The Value of Values, a Card Game Tool

Appendix 1

Pool of Generic Values[95]

Acceptance	Expertise	Respect
Accuracy	Freedom (Liberty)	Satisfaction
Achievement	Growth	Self-control (Composure)
Acknowledgement	Happiness (Joy)	Structure
Adaptability	Harmony	Support
Adventure	Honesty	Synergy
Affection	Humor	Teamwork
Appreciation	Independence	Thoughtfulness
Authenticity	Integrity	Trust
Belonging	Intelligence	Understanding
Candor	Knowledge	Usefulness
Care	Leadership	Wealth
Challenge	Logic	
Commitment	Mindfulness	
Compassion	Motivational	
Completion	Open-mindedness	
Contribution	Optimism (Hopefulness)	
Creativity	Passion	
Credibility	Playfulness	
Discipline	Pleasure	
Effectiveness	Preparedness	
Efficiency	Professionalism	
Empathy	Punctuality	
Encouragement	Realism	

---

[95] The list of values is taken from the 2011 Values Across Cultures (VAC) study that is being conducted in 30 countries across the globe by a team of researchers from ESADE under my general supervision. Values are listed in an alphabetical order.

Appendix 2

Blank Template of the 3Es Tri-axial Model

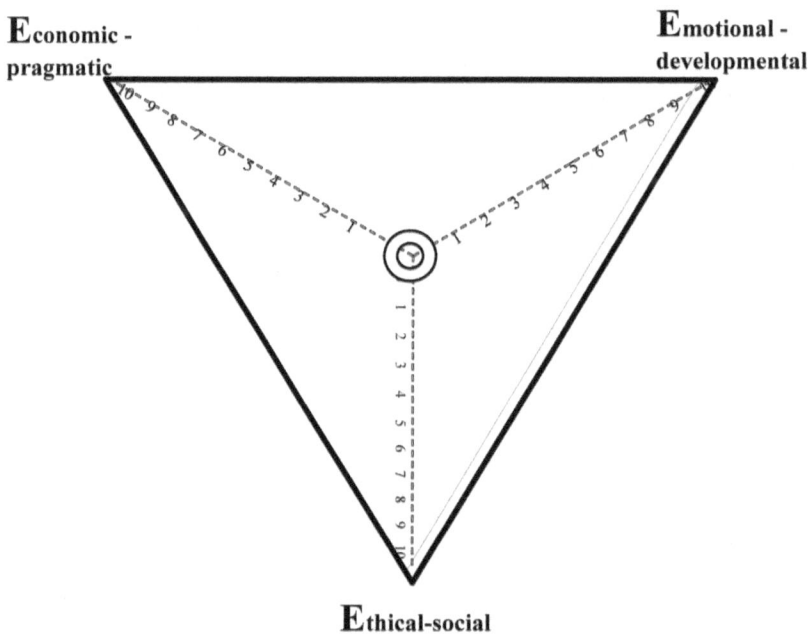

Appendix 3

The Value of Values, a Card Game Tool

As of summer 2011, there are four versions of the Value of Values card game in five languages (English, French, Spanish, Portuguese, and Hebrew). They can be found at *www.learning-about-values.com.* The card games are not simply translations; they have slight differences that reflect the cultures of the language in which the game was written.

The basic card game is currently available in four languages: English, Spanish, French, and Portuguese.

The Value of Values

www.learning-about-values.com

A special Spanish-language card game designed for Central Americans can be found at www.valoresenaccion.net.

For the Hebrew card game (Hebrew and English), go to www. equity-mds.com.

Simon L. Dolan

The Value of Values: Common denominator for all games

The Value of Values is a simple and enjoyable game that helps children and adults evaluate and prioritize their personal and shared values in a safe and supportive environment. It allows players to develop an understanding of the values that give significance to their actions and relationships and enable them to meaningfully and purposefully pursue their goals.

It is designed to initiate an open, deliberate, and safe dialogue about values through a playful and enjoyable experience. The cards are a tool to create the environment in which such a dialogue can take place.

Game play directs players through a process of identifying and prioritizing their own values, examining the influence of these values in their lives, and designing an action plan to narrow the gap between core values and actual behavior.

The Value of Values was developed by Simon Dolan and Avishai Landau and is based on the work of leading academics and researchers.

www.ingramcontent.com/pod-product-compliance
Lightning Source LLC
Chambersburg PA
CBHW031837170526
45157CB00001B/327